PRAISE FOR
LATERAL THINKING FOR EVERY DAY

"From outrageous ideas to weird combinations, Paul's unique approach to problem solving will revolutionize the way you think. Laterally the best book I've read this year."
Sam Kelly, Chief Marketing Officer, AKQA

"An enlightening read at a time when seeing the problem from multiple perspectives and finding creative solutions to move you forward has never been more important."
Tim Leney, Managing Director, TCC

"What a great read – highly entertaining and informative, packed with stories of real innovators and so many practical techniques."
Ralph Varcoe, Chief Growth Officer, Connexin

"This is the ultimate inspirational guide to lateral thinking, and a treasure trove for anyone interested in great stories about how taking a different perspective can grow yourself or your business – and having fun doing it."
Peter Hovstadius, former Chief Scientific Officer, Novartis Nordic RegionC

"Fascinating historic and current examples of lateral thinking."
Ian Gander, Managing Director, Gemini Data Loggers

"Paul Sloane has done it again. In his new book, he provides a number of simple frameworks and activities to build your teams' ability to think laterally, approach challenging problems in a new way and enhance their creativity."
Nick Skillicorn, innovation consultant and speaker

"Paul's very readable and entertaining presentation ably illustrates how you can use lateral thinking to benefit from changing perspectives and ideas in your home, social and business lives."
Dalim Basu, Chairman of London Branch,
British Computer Society

Lateral Thinking for Every Day

Extraordinary solutions to
ordinary problems

Paul Sloane

KoganPage

First published in Great Britain and the United States in 2023 by Kogan Page Limited

Apart from any fair dealing for the purposes of research or private study, or criticism or review, as permitted under the Copyright, Designs and Patents Act 1988, this publication may only be reproduced, stored or transmitted, in any form or by any means, with the prior permission in writing of the publishers, or in the case of reprographic reproduction in accordance with the terms and licences issued by the CLA. Enquiries concerning reproduction outside these terms should be sent to the publishers at the undermentioned addresses:

2nd Floor, 45 Gee Street	8 W 38th Street, Suite 902	4737/23 Ansari Road
London	New York, NY 10018	Daryaganj
EC1V 3RS	USA	New Delhi 110002
United Kingdom		India
www.koganpage.com		

ISBNs
Hardback   9781398607972
Paperback   9781398607941
Ebook   9781398607958

British Library Cataloguing-in-Publication Data
A CIP record for this book is available from the British Library.

Library of Congress Control Number
2022950033

Typeset by Hong Kong FIVE Workshop, Hong Kong
Print production managed by Jellyfish
Printed and bound by CPI Group (UK) Ltd, Croydon CR0 4YY

To six helpful lateral thinkers, my grandchildren:
Toby, Jerome, Madeleine, Arthur,
Frank and William

Contents

PART FIVE
Lateral thinking at work

About the author

Paul Sloane gained a first class degree in Engineering from Cambridge University. He came top of Sales School at IBM. He went on to become a Marketing Director, Managing Director and CEO of software companies. He is a leading speaker, author and consultant on lateral thinking and innovation. He has written over 20 books which have sold over two million copies in total. His top business book is *The Leader's Guide to Lateral Thinking Skills* (also published by Kogan Page). He runs leadership master classes on lateral thinking and innovation with corporations around the world. He has been a visiting lecturer at Cambridge University, Lancaster University, Henley Business School and the Mumbai Institute of Technology. His TEDx talk *Are You Open-Minded? Three Ways to Break Thinking Patterns* is available on YouTube. Paul is a keen player of golf, tennis and chess. He and his wife live in Camberley, England. They have three daughters and six grandchildren.

www.destination-innovation.com

Introduction

Lateral thinking is defined as the solving of problems by an indirect and creative approach, typically through viewing the problem from a different and unusual standpoint.

The phrase was coined by the Maltese doctor, psychologist and philosopher Edward de Bono in his 1967 book *The Use of Lateral Thinking*.[1] In the book he cites the biblical story of the Judgement of Solomon as an example of lateral thinking. Solomon was presented with two women who both claimed to be the mother of a child. Solomon provocatively suggested that the baby be cut in half and divided between the women. He carefully watched their reactions. One woman concurred with this idea but the second woman begged that the child be spared and given to her rival. Solomon judged the second woman to be the true mother.

Lateral thinking involves deliberately adopting an unconventional point of view in order to conceive unusual ideas and solutions. In his book *Sur/Petition*, de Bono tells how he was asked by the Ford Motor Company how they could differentiate themselves in the highly competitive car market.[2] His suggestion was that they buy a large car park company and make the car parks in city centres available for Ford cars only. The idea was too radical for Ford but it is a fine example of lateral thinking in action. They were thinking like automotive engineers while de Bono was thinking like a typical everyday driver who wants to be able to park in any city.

Why do we need lateral thinking? Because it is the key that unlocks creativity, innovation and fresh solutions to all sorts of problems, from climate change to café culture to deterring criminals. How can we harness the power of lateral thinking and apply it to everyday problems? That is the question that this book sets out to answer. It contains a catalogue of examples, methods, tricks and tactics that you can use to sidestep the obvious and find radical results.

It is written in short sharp chapters which are easy to read but contain plenty to digest. I have chosen examples, whether ancient or modern, that I believe best illustrate each aspect of lateral thinking.

We start by examining the dangers of conformity, group-think and conventional thinking. We then consider historical examples, techniques and methods, practical tips, lessons for business and lateral thinking in society.

If this book leads you to think differently and act differently then it has succeeded.

Part One
The basics

01

What is lateral thinking?

Edward de Bono used the term 'lateral thinking' in contrast to conventional or vertical thinking. In conventional thinking we go forward in a predictable, direct fashion. Lateral thinking involves coming at the problem from new directions – literally from the side. It enables us to conceive new possibilities and creative solutions to problems large and small. It is a fundamental component of innovation.

De Bono defined the four main aspects of lateral thinking as:

1 The recognition of dominant polarizing ideas.

2 The search for different ways of looking at things.

3 A relaxation of the rigid control of vertical thinking.

4 The use of chance.

There are dominant ideas in every walk of life. They are the assumptions, rules and conventions that underpin systems and influence people's thinking and attitudes. The idea that the Earth was flat or that the Earth was the centre of the Universe are examples of dominant ideas that polarized thought along set lines. Once the dominant ideas are in place then everything else is viewed in a way that supports them. Someone who is paranoid sees every attempt to help them as malevolent and manipulating. Someone who believes in a conspiracy theory will explain away any inconvenient facts as deliberately constructed by the powers behind the conspiracy. Most organizations have dominant ideas that polarize their view of the world. It is easy for us to be critical of the makers of horse-drawn carriages who thought that automobiles were silly contraptions that would never catch on. However, we are the captives of established ideas too.

A lateral thinking technique we can use is to write down all the dominant ideas that apply in our situation and then to deliberately challenge them. So for example the major airlines used to work with these beliefs:

- Customers want high standards of service.
- We issue tickets for all flights.
- We allocate seating in advance.
- We sell through travel agents.
- We fly to major airports because that is what business travellers want.

Of course, the low-cost airlines broke all of these rules and created a huge new market. A good start with lateral thinking is to deliberately turn every assumption and dominant idea on its head and see where that leads.

Asking 'What if?' is a lateral thinking technique that helps us to explore possibilities and challenge assumptions at the same time. We use the 'What if?' question to stretch every dimension of the issue. Each 'What if?' question should be extreme to the point of being ridiculous. Say we are running a small charity that cares for homeless dogs. The challenge is, 'How can we double our fund-raising income?' The sort of 'What if?' questions we could ask might be:

What if we had only one donor?

What if we had 10 million donors?

What if we had an unlimited marketing budget?

What if we had no marketing budget?

What if everyone had to look after a homeless dog for a day?

What if dogs slept in beds and people slept in kennels?

What if dogs could speak?

Start with a challenge and, individually or in a group, generate a short list of really provocative 'What if?' questions. Take one and see where it leads. Follow the crazy train of thought and see what emerges. You will start with silly ideas but these often lead to radical insights and innovations.

The role of chance in major inventions and scientific discoveries is well documented. The transmission of radio waves was discovered by Hertz when some of his equipment happened to produce a spark on the other side of the room. Alexander Fleming discovered penicillin when he noticed that one of his old Petri dishes had developed a mould that was resistant to bacteria. X-rays were discovered accidentally by Wilhelm Röntgen when he was playing with a cathode ray tube. Christopher Columbus discovered America when he was looking for a route to India. Pfizer developed a new drug for the treatment of angina but found in the tests that it had a remarkable side-effect on men; they had stumbled on to the drug now known as Viagra. The common theme is that someone with a curious mind sets out to investigate things. When something unusual happens, they study it and see how it can be put to use. The same methods can work for us. When we are looking for new ideas and fresh ways to do things then a random input can help us. A highly effective brainstorming technique is to take a noun at random from the dictionary. Write down some associations or attributes of the word and then force-fit connections between the word or its associations and the brainstorming challenge.

Lateral thinking will help you to become a much more effective problem solver, a more creative innovator and a more interesting person. It will enable you to generate many fresh, better ideas. And it can be great fun!

02
The dangers of conformity

Henri Tajfel was born in Poland in 1919. As a young man he left Poland because of restrictions on Jews in universities and went to France to study chemistry at the Sorbonne. At the start of the Second World War he volunteered to serve in the French army and was subsequently taken prisoner by the Germans. He survived the war in prisoner-of-war camps but on his return home he found that his family and most of his friends had died in the Nazi Holocaust. This had a deep effect on Tajfel and it led him to devote his life to the study of the psychology of prejudice and group relations.

After the war he moved to Britain and took British citizenship. He studied psychology at London University and in 1967 he became Chair of Social Psychology at the University of Bristol, where he carried out research into intergroup relations.

At that time, the common assumption among psychologists was that extreme prejudice was the result of extreme personality factors. Tajfel did not believe this. He had seen how large numbers of ordinary Germans, not just personality outliers, had supported the Nazis and their vicious policies towards Jews. Nazism had had the support of many Germans who would otherwise be considered normal. Tajfel thought that extreme prejudice might be the result of social group processes rather than extreme personality types. In a series of ground-breaking experiments in the 1970s he brought together groups of local boys. At first, boys preferred to be in a group with those around them rather than those further away. Tajfel went on to show that just putting people into groups was enough to cause them to discriminate in favour of their own group and against members of other groups. He found that the very act of categorization by itself produces conflict and discrimination.

Evolution has led us to crave groups. We were raised in tribes which supported and protected us. We want to fit in. Being part of a social group gives us a sense of belonging. There are many benefits to being in a group. The problem is that there is also a powerful force to conform to the ideas, standards and customs of the group.

Solomon Asch was born in 1907, also in Poland to a Jewish family. The family emigrated to the US in 1920. Asch became Professor of Psychology at Rutgers University, where he carried out a classic experiment to test conformity to group norms. In a series of trials, he put one unknowing student into a room with seven stooges who had been given instructions. The real participant thought that all eight people were genuine. They were then asked to compare the lengths of lines in two pictures.

Each person in the room had to state aloud which comparison line was most like the target line. The answer was always obvious but in some trials the stooges all gave the same wrong answer. The real participant sat at the end of the row and gave his or her answer last. Fully 75 per cent of the participants rejected the evidence of their own eyes and conformed to the views of the other people in the group.

Asch found that people conform for two main reasons: because they want to fit in with the group and because they believe the group is better informed than they are.

We support our local football club and disdain the opposition sides. We join groups at the golf club, the bridge club, the rotary club, the church and so on. In each case we conform to the norms, views and customs of the group.

We belong to groups on Twitter, Facebook, TikTok and LinkedIn. The wide range of social media sites and contributors should mean that we read a wide variety of opinions, but the opposite is generally the case. People dwell in echo chambers where they read posts which reinforce their own views, opinions and prejudices. This can lead to polarization which can become extreme. Think of the Trump supporters who believed, in the face of all the evidence, that the 2020 election was stolen from him. Or the extreme views of the Covid anti-vaxxers.

Because we are all prey to the forces of group conformity, we need lateral thinking. We must be able to challenge the assumptions and attitudes that everyone else takes for granted. We need to be open-minded and curious. This approach can bear a cost. The lateral thinker is often seen as a heretic, an outsider, a non-conformist. But the benefits can be manifold in freeing our thinking and enabling us to find new, better ideas. We can escape the straitjacket of the crowd.

The lateral thinker is aware of the dangers of obvious thinking. They are on the lookout for ways to combat the tendency to slip into conformity. They strive to sidestep the obvious and find a better and less-trodden path.

03

Fight the menace of groupthink

One of the most common obstacles to effective decision making by teams is groupthink. The term is used to describe the observation that many people when in a group make poor decisions because they try to reach a consensus and minimize conflict. In doing so they suppress dissenting viewpoints, eschew controversial issues and isolate themselves from outside influences. The result is that they do not seriously consider alternatives to the group's view.

A much-discussed example of groupthink is the Bay of Pigs fiasco in 1961. The Kennedy administration uncritically accepted the CIA plan to invade Cuba. They ignored dissenting voices and outside opinion and underestimated the obstacles. President Kennedy learnt from this disaster. During the Cuban Missile Crisis in 1962 he used 'vigilant appraisal' to deliberately avoid groupthink. He invited outside experts to share their viewpoints. He encouraged group members to voice opinions, ask questions and challenge assumptions. The President purposely absented himself from some meetings to prevent his opinions dominating.

President Nixon's advisers knew that the actions he proposed in the Watergate incident were risky and illegal, but they did not dare gainsay him.

A more recent example is given by Matthew Syed in his book *Rebel Ideas*.[3] He explains how the CIA missed the threat of Osama Bin Laden and the 9/11 attacks because of groupthink. The CIA recruited the top graduates from Yale and Harvard but employed pitifully few Arabic speakers or Muslims. CIA employees were highly intelligent, but they lacked cognitive diversity. They thought the same way. They could not conceive that a man living in a cave in Afghanistan could present a viable threat to the US.

The accounting fraud which led to the collapse of Enron in 2001, the bankruptcy of Swissair in 2002 and the Volkswagen emissions scandal of 2015 have all been blamed on groupthink. In each case senior executives went along with disastrous plans because they were loyal, aligned and reluctant to question the leader.

The phenomenon of groupthink was researched in the 1970s by Irving Janis, a research psychologist at Yale University. He identified various causes including the desire for cohesiveness, lack of impartial leadership, homogeneity of the group members and stressful external threats.

In his seminal book on the topic, *Groupthink*,[4] Janis recommends eight ways to prevent groupthink:

- Leaders should assign each member the role of 'critical evaluator'. This allows each member to freely air objections and doubts.

- Leaders should not express an opinion when assigning a task to a group.

- Leaders should absent themselves from many of the group meetings to avoid excessively influencing the outcome.

- The organization should set up several independent groups, working on the same problem.

- All effective alternatives should be examined.

- Each member should discuss the group's ideas with trusted people outside of the group.

- The group should invite outside experts into meetings. Group members should be allowed to discuss with and question the outside experts.

- At least one group member should be assigned the role of devil's advocate. This should be a different person for each meeting.

The countless examples of groupthink in teams should give us pause to ponder. It suppresses lateral thinking and radical alternatives. Leaders of groups and meetings can avoid groupthink misfortunes by learning from the actions of Kennedy and the prescriptions of Janis.

04
Contemplate the opposite

When you want to make progress the obvious thing to do is to adapt and improve the current system or product. The lateral thinker goes way beyond this approach. They contemplate doing the opposite.

In the 1930s there were 2,000 salesmen in the US knocking on doors and selling sets of the *Encyclopaedia Britannica*. They were selling a highly regarded product and were on handsome commissions. By the year 2000 the set comprised 32 volumes of carefully researched entries provided by 100 full-time editors and 4,000 contributors. First published in Edinburgh in 1768, *Encyclopaedia Britannica* became a trusted reference work in homes, schools and offices around the world. But in 2012 the print edition ceased production. Why did the company halt the presses after 244 years?

The work had become very expensive to produce and difficult to keep up to date. In the 1990s Microsoft launched a CD-ROM product, Encarta, which was nowhere near as accurate or comprehensive as the *Encyclopaedia Britannica*, but it was very cheap and it included a search function. Encarta was discontinued in 2009 by which time a new and mighty competitor was dominating the market – Wikipedia.

Wikipedia was founded by Jimmy Wales and Larry Sanger in 2001 as a web-based, free encyclopaedia. It was constructed on a remarkably lateral idea. They employed an open-door policy which allowed anyone to create and edit articles on the site. Initially this meant that any article could contain inaccuracies such as errors, biases and irrelevant text. Gradually editing restrictions and controls were introduced. The content is largely self-policed by a community of volunteers. By 2019 Wikipedia had nearly six million articles in English and was also available in 300 other languages.

In this case the opposite of expensive was not inexpensive; it was free. The opposite of 100 paid editors was not 10 paid editors; it was thousands of unpaid editors. The result was a living body of work which was constantly updated and enhanced. Many people scoffed at the original notion of Wikipedia. They pointed out that there was no guarantee that any article was unbiased or accurate and that there was no sustainable business model to monetize the site and generate revenue. Despite these reasonable (but conventional) concerns, Wikipedia has flourished and is now the largest and most popular reference work on the World Wide Web.

Innovation means doing something different and what could be more different than the exact opposite? If your current plans and policies are not working, then try doing the opposite.

The policy of all major software companies such as Microsoft, Oracle and IBM was to protect their intellectual property. Only a handful of loyal employees were allowed access to the full source code of major software programs and steps were taken to ensure that the valuable programming secrets never left the company's site. Linus Torvalds, a Finnish programmer, decided to do the opposite. He created an operating system, Linux, so that anybody could view and amend the source code. This meant that anybody could effectively own and change the software. It was difficult if not impossible to control but that did not worry him because it also unleashed a wave of free creativity and innovation. He created the open-source movement by doing the opposite of all the big players.

The Artist won the Best Picture award at the 2012 Oscars. It was a silent movie. The director had deliberately opposed conventional movie-making by filming in black and white and without big stars, computer-assisted scenes or even spoken dialogue.

Jean-Claude Killy was a French downhill skier who wanted to win gold in a Winter Olympics. But he could not do it using the conventional methods so he did the opposite. Everyone was coached to keep their skis together and their weight forward going downhill. He created a new style called *avalement* which involved keeping the skis apart and sitting back on them. Killy won three gold medals at the 1968 Olympics.

When Anita Roddick founded the Body Shop retail chain she did the opposite of her major rivals. They all presented their perfumes and shampoos in expensive bottles and plush packaging. She used cheap plastic bottles and simple packaging to stress that the contents were what mattered – and they were pure and simple.

More recent examples include Uber, a taxi company which does not own a single taxi. Or Airbnb, a hotel company which does not own a single hotel. Or Turo, a car rental company which does not own a single car. They evince the exact opposite of conventional approaches.

We are all plagued by emails from scam artists who tell us we have won the lottery or can help them move millions out of some obscure bank account. The conventional advice is to ignore these emails. But what if we did the opposite? What if we all responded by asking for more details? The scammers, who send out millions of emails, would be overwhelmed and unable to cope.

Look at your current policies and strategies. Look at your underlying assumptions. Ask yourself, 'What if the opposite were true?' Don't just consider something different. Go further and contemplate the exact opposite.

05
Break the rules

On 26 September 1983, the Russian OKO early-warning
system signalled that six missiles had been launched from
the US and they were heading for the USSR. Soviet
military protocol dictated that this warning should be
immediately reported to senior officials in Moscow. The
officer on duty was Lieutenant Colonel Stanislav Petrov. He
made a momentous decision. He judged the report to be a
false alarm and did not alert Moscow. Had he done so it is
quite possible that it would have triggered a retaliatory
nuclear attack on the US. He reasoned that it was unlikely
that the US would launch an attack with just six missiles. It
was subsequently shown that the Soviet satellite warning
system had failed. The false alarm had been caused by a rare
alignment of sunlight on clouds. Petrov broke the rules. He
disobeyed orders. It is likely that he saved the world from a
devastating nuclear war.

In the 1970s IBM dominated the mainframe computer
arena but smaller companies were springing up fast with
mini-computers and home computers. The company asked
Don Estridge to develop an inexpensive personal computer
to take on the upstarts like Atari, Apple and Commodore.
At that time IBM maintained total control of all its manufacturing with proprietary designs from power supplies to inte-
grated circuits to operating systems. Estridge decided to
break all the rules of standard procedure and instead to go

outside the company for third-party components and software. Even more radically Estridge opted for an 'open architecture'. He published the specifications of the IBM PC, thus enabling a burgeoning industry of suppliers of add-ons, hardware and software products. In 1981, within one year of development, the IBM PC was on retail shelves, a record time for product development in the giant company. The IBM PC was a huge success and quickly came to dominate the market.

Muhammad Yunus is a Bangladeshi banker and economist who broke the rules of banking to develop the concepts of microcredit and microfinance. Typically, banks would only make loans at a minimum level of hundreds of dollars. They would only lend to people with good credit ratings and they would ask for some collateral as security against the loan. In 1983 Yunus's bank, Grameen, started giving tiny loans with no security to entrepreneurs too poor to qualify for traditional bank loans. Despite strong opposition from critics the scheme was a great success and millions of small loans were made. Over 90 per cent of the loans were to women and the default rate was less than 3 per cent. In 2006 Yunus received the Nobel Peace Prize for this innovation which has transformed social and economic development in Bangladesh and other parts of the developing world.

Freddie Mercury wrote 'Bohemian Rhapsody' and Queen released it in 1975. He had started developing ideas for the song in the 1960s. He did not write it to please customers or to follow a formula for a hit record. He wrote it as creative piece of self-indulgent musical expression.

The song broke all the rules for a popular music single release. At a time when most pop songs were simple and formulaic Mercury's song was a complex mixture of different styles and tempos. It had six separate sections – a close-harmony a capella introduction, a ballad, a guitar solo, an opera parody, a rock anthem and a melodic finale. It contained enigmatic and fatalistic lyrics about killing a man. And it was very long.

When it was proposed to Queen's record company, EMI, that they release the song as a single they flatly rejected the idea. It was 5 minutes 55 seconds in duration and the general rule of the day was that radio stations only played items that lasted no more than three and a half minutes.

So Queen bypassed EMI and went straight to the DJ Kenny Everett. They gave him a copy on condition that he only play sections of it. He did this and the sections intensified audience reaction and desire. When the shops opened on the following Monday morning hordes of fans went into music stores to buy the record only to be told that it was not available. EMI was forced to release it and the song that they claimed was unplayable went on to become one of their greatest hits. It was the first song to reach number one twice with the same version – in 1975 on its first release and in 1991 following Mercury's death. It went gold in the US with over a million copies sold. It had a worldwide resurgence in 1992 when it featured in the film *Wayne's World*. In 2002 it was named by *Guinness World Records* as the top British single of all time.

A key precept of lateral thinking is to challenge conventions. This means questioning assumptions and it often leads the lateral thinker to break the rules of their game and even to disobey orders. This is clearly risky but sometimes it leads to a hit record or to saving the world.

06
Think like an outsider

What do the following people have in common? Levi Strauss, Henry Ford, Estee Lauder, Walt Disney, Elon Musk, Arianna Huffington, Sergey Brin, Will Shu (founder of Deliveroo) and Jan Koum (founder of WhatsApp)? They are all famous entrepreneurs who founded successful new businesses. But also, they are all immigrants or the children of immigrants.

In *You Only Have To be Right Once*, Randall Lane gives many examples of immigrants who have launched successful businesses.[5] Pejman Nozad fled from Iran and in 1992 arrived in the US speaking no English and with only $700. He got a job in San Francisco selling expensive Persian rugs. Many of his customers were rich and successful business-people from Silicon Valley. He built up a powerful network of contacts. He became a venture capitalist and founded Pear VC. By 2020 his companies had a valuation of over $20 billion.

Another example from the book is Don Chang who emigrated from South Korea to the US in 1981 at the age of 18. With little English and no college degree, he worked in coffee shops. He became interested in fashion and saved to set up his own store. He and his wife, Jin Sook, used just $11,000 in savings to open a clothing store called Fashion 21 in 1984 in Los Angeles. The shop was a success, they expanded to other locations and changed the business name to Forever 21. By 2015 they had 600 shops and 30,000 employees.

According to the Entrepreneurs Network, while just 14 per cent of UK residents are foreign-born, 49 per cent of the UK's fastest-growing start-ups have at least one foreign-born co-founder.[6]

The Kauffman Organization reports that more than 40 per cent of Fortune 500 companies were founded by immigrants or their children, over 50 per cent of American billion-dollar 'unicorn' start-ups have at least one immigrant founder, and immigrants are nearly twice as likely as the native-born to start a new company.[7]

Immigrants have been awarded 37 per cent of the Nobel Prizes won by Americans in chemistry, medicine and physics since 2000, according to an analysis by the National Foundation for American Policy.[8]

Many other studies show similar results. Why are immigrants better than natives when it comes to innovation, invention and entrepreneurship? It is mainly what Matthew Syed calls the 'outsider mindset'. They have experienced a different country and a different culture. They have not grown up with the assumptions and beliefs which are ingrained in most of the population. Because they are outside the normal frame of reference they can challenge the status quo and see new possibilities. They can contrast and combine two different viewpoints because that is what they have done since their arrival.

Whenever I meet someone from one country living in another I ask them this question: 'What did you notice as being odd or different about the culture of your new home country?' The answers are often surprising. I asked a German businessman living in Portugal this question. He replied, 'In

Germany if you schedule a business meeting for 9 am, everyone is there at 9 am. In Portugal, people start appearing at 9.15.' He told me other things that he and his wife had spotted as very different from Germany. Things which the locals would take for granted but an immigrant would notice as odd.

When we are immersed in a topic, in a business or in a way of life we are surrounded by its conventions and limitations. We can become trapped in our way of thinking. The outsider can bring an open mind to the situation and a fresh point of view. If you are not an immigrant, then try to think like one. Mix with outsiders and ask them to comment frankly. Or maybe employ some immigrants to benefit from their diverse viewpoints and ideas.

07
Ask dumb questions

The lateral thinker is always curious. They ask a great many questions – smart questions, dumb questions, basic questions, childlike questions.

In 1970, Roger Hargreaves' six-year-old son Adam asked his father a question. It was a question only a child could ask; no adult would ever conceive of it. Adam said, 'Daddy, what does a tickle look like?'

In response Hargreaves, a cartoonist, drew a picture of a round orange blob with a face and long rubbery arms. It became the central character in his first book, *Mr Tickle*. He had difficulty finding a publisher willing to take it on but eventually the book was published and went on to be the start of the Mr Men series which have sold over 90 million copies. They are favourites of children all over the world.

Hargreaves was the Creative Director at a London agency but in 1976 he left his job to concentrate on his writing. He and his wife had four children but in 1988 he died at the age of 53 following a stroke.

His great creations came because he listened to what on first hearing sounds like a very silly question. One which Mr Silly might have asked. But silly questions challenge conventional ideas and prompt lateral thinking.

Children learn by asking questions. Students learn by asking questions. New recruits learn by asking questions. When you started your last job, you asked a lot of questions. It is the simplest and most effective way of learning. But after a while you probably stopped asking questions. Most people ask fewer questions as they get older and more experienced. Lateral thinkers never stop asking questions because they know that this is the best way to gain deeper insights.

According to a newspaper report children ask their parents some 73 questions a day, many of which the parents struggle to answer.[9] Alistair Cox, CEO of Hays Group, believes that adults ask around 20 questions a day.[10] Children ask questions to learn about and understand the world but according to the *Independent* article a child's inquisitiveness peaks at age four and then declines.

Eric Schmidt, when CEO of Google, said, 'We run this company on questions, not answers.' He knew that if you employ smart people, they can find smart answers if only you can find the right questions to give them.

The great TV detective Columbo solves his mysteries by asking many questions. All the great inventors and scientists asked questions. Isaac Newton asked, 'Why does an apple fall from a tree?' and 'Why does the Moon not fall into the Earth?' Charles Darwin asked, 'Why do the Galapagos Islands have so many species not found elsewhere?' Albert Einstein asked, 'What would the universe look like if I rode through it on a beam of light?' By asking these kinds of fundamental questions they were able to start the process that led to their tremendous breakthroughs.

Why do we stop asking questions? Some people assume they know all the main things they need to know and they do not bother to ask more. They cling to established beliefs and remain certain in their assumptions – yet the world is constantly changing around them. Things that were true yesterday are no longer true today.

Some people are afraid that by asking questions they will look weak, ignorant or unsure. They prefer to appear decisive and sure of themselves. But smart leaders know that asking questions is a sign of strength, not weakness. Some people are so busy that they do not pause to ask questions – they rush straight to action. But they might be trying to solve the wrong problem.

As a lateral thinker you should be prepared to question everything. Start with very basic, broad questions, then move to more specific areas to clarify your understanding. Good questions that you might ask in business are:

- What are we trying to achieve here?
- Why do customers buy our product or service?
- What problem do we solve?
- Is there a better way to provide this service?

As we listen to answers, further questions spring to mind. For each response we can ask 'Why?' When someone gives an answer, we can often ask, 'Why?' As we keep asking question so our understanding of the issue deepens and we gain fresh insights for creative solutions.

A powerful lateral thinking technique in a group is to ask 'What if' questions. Nothing is off limits with the question and they can stretch the parameters of the problem in extreme directions, e.g.

- What if we only had one customer?
- What if we had 10 million customers
- What if we had an unlimited marketing budget?
- What if we had no marketing budget?

- What if were bought by Disney Corporation?
- What if our new CEO was Lady Gaga?

You choose one of these questions and see where it takes you. You will conceive any manner of crazy ideas – one of which may turn into a winner.

Be childlike. Ask more questions. Ask basic questions. Ask smart questions. Ask seemingly dumb questions to really challenge assumptions.

Part Two
Historical examples

08
Seven companies that switched

Peter Drucker famously said, 'Every organization must prepare for the abandonment of everything it does.'[11] Here are examples of seven successful companies which switched from one activity to another in order to meet a customer need.

Tiffany was started in 1837 by Charles Tiffany and John Young, in Brooklyn, Connecticut, as a 'stationery and fancy goods emporium'. In 1862, during the Civil War, the company supplied the Union Army with swords, flags and surgical implements. After the war Tiffany focused on jewellery. It is now renowned for its luxury goods and opulent stores. Tiffany was acquired by LVMH (Louis Vuitton) in 2021 for $16 billlion.

Berkshire Hathaway was originally a textile manufacturing company established by Oliver Chace in 1839 in Rhode Island. The company went through many mergers and acquisitions in textiles but by the 1950s this old textile business was in decline and cutting back. A young entrepreneur, Warren Buffett, began buying stock in Berkshire Hathaway after noticing that the stock price fell whenever the company closed a mill. In 1962 he became the majority owner in this failing textile business. He used it as a vehicle to buy stakes in insurance companies and other businesses. By astute investing, Buffett grew the business in astounding fashion and Berkshire Hathaway became the largest financial services conglomerate in the world. In 2022 it had a market capitalization of over $700 billion.

Nokia was founded in 1865 by mining engineer Fredrik Idestam as a wood pulp mill in Tampere, Finland, which was then part of the Russian Empire. It became a manufacturer of rubber boots and cables before specializing in electronics. In the 1990s it focused on telecommunications technology. From 1998 to 2008 it was the world's largest supplier of mobile phones and smartphones but fell behind Apple and Samsung. It became a network equipment manufacturer.

Avon was founded by David McConnell in New York in 1886. Initially the business sold books door to door. McConnell gave samples of perfume as an incentive for book sales but found that demand for the perfume exceeded that for the books. He went on to focus on perfumes and cosmetics and built the Avon brand and empire based on an army of 'Avon Ladies' selling direct to customers.

Nintendo was started in 1889 as Fusajiro Yamauchi as a company producing Japanese hanafuda playing cards. Nintendo produced its first console, the Color TV-Game, in 1977. It gained international success with its game Donkey Kong in 1981 and with Super Mario Bros in 1985. It has gone on to sell a range of highly successful video game consoles including Game Boy, the Super Nintendo Entertainment System and the Wii.

In 1891, a 29-year-old businessman, William Wrigley Jr, began a company in Chicago selling scouring soap and baking powder. As an incentive he offered two packets of chewing gum for each purchase of a can of baking powder. The chewing gum proved more popular than the baking powder, so Wrigley switched his focus to gum. The Wrigley Company is now the largest manufacturer and marketer of chewing gum in the world. In 2008 Mars Inc acquired Wrigley's for $23 billion.

The toy company Hasbro was originally founded by three Polish Jewish brothers, as Hassenfeld Brothers in Providence, Rhode Island, in 1923. The company sold textile remnants. The firm expanded to produce pencil cases and school supplies. They started selling toys in the 1940s and their first major success was called Mr Potato Head. The company now has revenues of over $5 billion and its products include Transformers, G.I. Joe, Power Rangers, Micronauts, Monopoly, Furby, Nerf, Twister and My Little Pony.

The lesson is clear. Find something that customers like and that you are good at. If that means shifting completely from today's business model, then so be it. Lateral thinking sometimes involves a complete turnaround.

09

Why do experts reject new ideas?

We would expect scientists, doctors and experts to be open-minded and receptive to new ideas. But there are many examples of where highly trained people clung to outdated assumptions and rejected new ideas despite strong evidence for their efficacy.

Ignaz Semmelweis (1818–1865) was a Hungarian doctor and scientist who worked at a time when puerperal fever (also known as childbirth fever) was common in hospital maternity wards and often fatal. Semmelweis worked at the Vienna General Hospital's Obstetric Clinic, where he learnt that doctors' wards had three times the mortality of midwives' wards. He found that the incidence of this condition could be greatly reduced by rigorous hand washing by clinicians dealing with childbirth. In 1847 he proposed that doctors and nurses should wash their hands with a chlorinated lime solution. The medical community of the day was offended. They rejected the idea that their contaminated hands could possibly be responsible for the deaths of patients. He struggled on against outspoken attacks but in 1865 he suffered a breakdown. His medical colleagues had him committed to an asylum where he was beaten by the guards and died.

It was years after his death that the work of Louis Pasteur and Joseph Lister showed that antiseptic cleansing could combat the deadly effects of germs, thus vindicating Semmelweis's approach. He is now recognized as an early pioneer of antiseptic procedures. He has been called the 'saviour of mothers'.

Alfred Wegener (1880–1930) was a German climatologist, geologist and meteorologist who is celebrated as the originator of the theory of continental drift. He conceived this idea when he noticed that the different large landmasses of the Earth fitted together as though they were parts of a jigsaw puzzle. The continental shelf of the Americas fits closely to Africa and Europe. Similarly, Antarctica, Australia, India and Madagascar fit next to the tip of Southern Africa. He analysed rock types and fossils on both sides of the Atlantic Ocean and found significant similarities. He published his theory in 1912, contending that all the continents were once joined together in a single landmass and had since drifted apart. This idea was met with scepticism and stoutly resisted by leading professional geologists of the day, who considered Wegener to be an outsider. The American Association of Petroleum Geologists held a symposium specifically in opposition to the continental drift hypothesis.

Wegener died on an expedition to Greenland in 1930 when he was 50. His ideas were not accepted until the 1950s, when discoveries based on the new science of palaeomagnetism vindicated Wegener's theory of continental drift. This led to current models of plate tectonics. Subsequently the use of Global Positioning System (GPS) has enabled the accurate measurement of continental drift.

Per-Ingvar Brånemark (1929–2014) was a Swedish physician and research professor, acknowledged as the father of modern dental implantology. In 1952, when he was 23, Brånemark made a remarkable discovery – by accident. He was researching bone marrow, and, in an experiment, he implanted a piece of titanium into the leg bone of a living rabbit. After some time, he tried to remove the piece of metal but found that it had become fused with the bone. The fusion of titanium and bone was a previously unknown biological process. Brånemark called it osseointegration but he did not immediately see an application for it. Eleven years later, in 1963, a dentist colleague asked him to meet Gosta Larsson, a 34-year-old man who had been born with a cleft palate and deformed lower jaw. He had no teeth in his lower jaw and could not chew food. Dentists had been unable to solve this problem. Brånemark suggested that they fix titanium screws in the man's jawbone to which artificial teeth could be attached. Larsson agreed and the whole operation proved a remarkable success. The implants worked well and without trouble for the remaining 40 years of Larsson's life.

Brånemark successfully carried out similar procedures on other patients who had severe dental difficulties. However, dentists strongly rejected this approach and were highly critical of Brånemark – partly because he was not a dentist but an outsider in their community. In 1973 a meeting of the Swedish National On tological Assembly roundly condemned Brånemark's methods and he received many nasty personal criticisms. In 1974 a group of irate dentists petitioned the National Board of Health to ban all procedures involving osseointegration. The Board carried out an investigation and found the Brånemark's treatments were highly effective and safe.

Eventually dentists in Europe and then North America were convinced, and dental implants became standard procedure. Brånemark received many awards and belated recognition for his contribution to dentistry and public health.

It is a curious fact that the best educated people are often the ones most resistant to fresh ideas. It seems that once they have learnt a method or adopted a theory it becomes an orthodoxy that they are reluctant to see challenged. Lateral thinkers often have to suffer criticism or even ridicule before their unorthodox ideas are accepted.

10
Fly, crash, adapt

Paul MacCready (1925–2007) was an aeronautical engineer and lateral thinker. He invented the first human-powered aircraft. MacCready was born in Connecticut to a family of doctors. He was fascinated by engineering and aeroplanes from a young age. At 15 he won a national model building contest. He said, 'I was always the smallest kid in the class and certainly not the athlete type. And so, when I began getting into model aeroplanes, and getting into contests and creating new things, I probably got more psychological benefit from that than I would have from some of the other typical school things.'

MacCready trained as a US Navy pilot during the Second World War. He gained a degree in physics from Yale University and a PhD in aeronautics from the California Institute of Technology. In 1951 MacCready founded his first company, Meteorology Research, to carry out atmospheric research. He was a pioneer in the use of aircraft to study meteorological phenomena.

He was an expert glider and won a national contest for gliding three times between 1948 and 1953. In 1956 he became the World Soaring Champion. He was an inventor and came up with a device that optimized speed choices for glider pilots, depending on conditions. It is still in use.

In the 1970s, he invested in a business which failed, leaving him with a $100,000 debt. This motivated him to enter the Kremer competition which offered a reward for the first human-powered flight.

The Kremer Prize had been set up in 1959 by British industrialist Henry Kremer. It promised £50,000 in prize money to the first group that could fly a human-powered aircraft over a figure-8 course covering a total of one mile and including certain height markers. Early efforts to build human-powered aircraft had featured wooden designs, which proved too heavy. Some used catapults to launch the craft. Different British teams had achieved limited success with distance but struggled to steer their craft around the course. The prize stood unclaimed for 18 years.

Paul MacCready and Peter Lissaman took a fresh look at the challenge. They came up with an unorthodox design they called the Gossamer Condor. It was based on hang gliders with a very large wing area and a gondola underneath for the pilot. It featured a novel control mechanism called a canard ahead of the main fuselage. The craft was built of lightweight plastics, bicycle parts and aluminium spars. It was capable of taking off under human power.

The Gossamer Condor was designed to be easily modified and repaired after the many crashes which it suffered in development. At one stage the tail flap was adjusted by taping a piece of card to it. There were many evolutions.

Eventually on 23 August 23 1977 the aircraft, piloted by Bryan Allen, stayed aloft for seven minutes and completed the figure-8 course specified by the Royal Aeronautical Society, at Minter Field in Shafter, California. The prize was won.

The Gossamer Condor is preserved at the Smithsonian National Air and Space Museum.

Kremer offered a further £100,000 for the first human-powered crossing of the English Channel. MacCready accepted the challenge. In 1979, he built the Condor's successor, the Gossamer Albatross, and with it he won the second Kremer prize, successfully flying from England to France. For his design and construction of the Albatross, MacCready was awarded the Collier Trophy, an annual prize for the greatest achievement in aeronautics.

In 1971 he founded AeroVironment, a public company that developed unmanned aircraft. It built the first aeroplane to be powered by hydrogen fuel cells, the Global Observer. He went on to design and build solar-powered aircraft such as the Gossamer Penguin and the Solar Challenger. He worked with NASA on solar-powered aircraft and with General Motors on the design of a solar-powered car.

In 1985, he built a half-scale working replica of the pterosaur Quetzalcoatlus for the Smithsonian Institution. The remote-controlled flying reptile had a wingspan of 18 feet. It flew successfully several times before crashing at an airshow in Maryland. MacCready helped to sponsor the Nissan Dempsey/MacCready Prize for innovations in racing-bicycle technology and faster human-powered vehicles. He died in 2007 from a melanoma.

The lateral thinker can take this motto from MacCready: Fly, Crash, Adapt. Other contestants spent years designing and building sophisticated aircraft which failed to win the prize. MacCready's team won in months. Part of their secret was the use of a fast feedback loop. They flew, they crashed, they adapted the plane. Failure was expected and used as source of learning and improvement. When we learn to ride a bicycle, we expect to fall off a few times. Despite the advocates of power of positive thinking we should not plan for success. We should expect our experiments to fail and then adapt after each crash.

Another lesson is to fly close to the ground. MacCready's craft and pilot could crash safely because they were never more than 15 feet above ground. Design your experiments so that you can fail safely.

11
We need to listen to contrarian thinkers

Henry Charles Keith Petty-Fitzmaurice (1845–1927), the fifth Marquess of Lansdowne, was a distinguished British statesman who held senior positions in both Liberal Party and Conservative Party governments. He had served as the fifth Governor General of Canada, Viceroy of India, Secretary of State for War and Secretary of State for Foreign Affairs. He was a pillar of the British aristocracy, steeped in the values of the establishment.

In November 1917 the First World War had raged for three savage years with millions of dead. Lansdowne, whose son had been killed in action, became convinced that the war was a threat to civilization itself and that the total destruction of Germany was not a worthwhile objective. Impelled by his conscience, he circulated a paper to the Government, in which he called for an end to the bloodshed and a negotiated peace with Germany. His proposal was summarily rejected by his colleagues. He invited the editor of *The Times*, Geoffrey Dawson, to his house and asked him to publish a letter expounding his case. Dawson was 'appalled' and refused. Lansdowne then offered the letter to the *Daily Telegraph*, which published it on 29 November 1917. It stated:

We are not going to lose this war, but its prolongation will spell ruin for the civilized world, and an infinite addition to the load of human suffering which already weighs upon it... We do not desire the annihilation of Germany as a great power... We do not seek to impose upon her people any form of government other than that of their own choice... We have no desire to deny Germany her place among the great commercial communities of the world.

Condemnation was swift and almost universal. Lansdowne became a pariah who was shunned and vilified by politicians, commentators and military leaders. His letter was condemned as a 'deed of shame'. It was completely at odds with popular opinion which wanted nothing less than the annihilation of Germany. His career was over and he was seen by many as a traitor. In the face of such opprobrium he maintained his views but they had no effect.

Most likely he was right. His views should have been considered. If peace could have been negotiated with Germany countless lives would have been saved. Furthermore the onerous reparations forced on Germany after the Treaty of Versailles in 1919 would have been avoided. Many historians believe that the terms of this treaty laid the seeds for the rise of Hitler and the horrors of the Second World War.

A parallel story occurred half a century after Lansdowne wrote his letter. Konrad Kellen (1913–2007) was a German Jew who studied law before emigrating to the US in 1935. He had a brilliant mind and became an intelligence officer working for the US army and later for the RAND Corporation, an influential think tank started by the Pentagon to perform high-level defence analysis. In the 1960s he studied interviews with hundreds of captured Viet Cong fighters in order to interpret the morale and intentions of North Vietnam. Conventional wisdom in the Pentagon was that the morale of the Viet Cong forces was low and that additional US forces and bombing would shortly bring about Viet Cong collapse.

Kellen's painstaking analysis led him to conclude that, contrary to prevailing assessments, enemy morale was high and that the war was not winnable. In 1965 he and others wrote an open letter to the US Government urging withdrawal of troops. His arguments were disregarded by the US Administration which maintained its optimistic view that the war was winnable because of low enemy morale. With hindsight we can see that Kellen was right and many lives would have been saved if his approach had been adopted. Why did he get it right and so many other advisers get it wrong? Author Malcolm Gladwell notes that Kellen was a truly great listener who could listen objectively without filtering what he heard through biases or predispositions.[12]

We can easily forget how difficult it is to voice an opinion contrary to the universal view. There have been many cases where whistle-blowers in government bodies, hospitals and large organizations have faced tremendous hostility and opposition even when acting in the public interest.

It takes great courage to challenge the powerful and the popular. We need that courage time and again. We should not disdain and ignore contrarian thinkers like Lansdowne and Kellen. They should be encouraged to speak up and their views, however unpopular, should be examined with dispassion.

In choosing to speak out against conventional thinking you must take care with your timing, method and manner. You can look arrogant or even manic. Gather the evidence and brief some allies in advance who will support you. Show that you are aligned with the goals of the organization or body and then express your concern that the current approach might not be for the best. Advance your argument with stories, facts, logic, emotion and humility.

12
Lateral thinking at war

Warfare is mankind's most serious endeavour. Tremendous efforts and forces are deployed in the struggle for victory or survival. But superior forces do not guarantee success. There has always been scope for agility and clever tactics to out-manoeuvre an enemy – remember David and Goliath. Here are some notable examples of lateral thinking in warfare.

The Wooden Horse of Troy

The Iliad is one of the oldest works of literature in Western civilization. It is an epic Greek poem written in the 8th century BC and attributed to Homer. It tells the tale of the long war between the Greeks and the Empire of Troy and the long siege of the city of Troy.

According to the legend, after an unsuccessful siege which lasted ten years, the Greeks led by Odysseus did some lateral thinking and constructed a huge wooden horse. They hid an elite force of some 40 men inside the horse. The huge Greek army then appeared to sail away having given up the fight. The jubilant Trojans pulled the horse into their city as a trophy. That night the Greek soldiers crept out of the horse and opened the gates to allow in the whole Greek army, which had sailed back under cover of night. The Greeks seized and sacked the mighty city of Troy, thus winning the war.

The term 'Trojan horse' has come to mean any deception that causes a target to accept a disguised enemy into a previously secure place.

Hannibal crossing the Alps

In 218 BC the 29-year-old Carthaginian general Hannibal set out on an audacious attack on the Roman Empire, the world's most dominant power. He led a large army from Spain, across southern France and through the Alps to attack the Roman Empire from the north. His army included 38 battle-trained elephants, a weapon the Roman soldiers had never seen before. No one had tried to march an army through the Alps before and Hannibal lost many soldiers to attacks, cold and avalanches but when he reached Italy he caught the Romans completely unawares.

The Romans sent armies to repel the Carthaginians but Hannibal defeated them in three great battles. The third of these is famous for the innovative tactics he deployed. At the battle of Cannae in 216 BC Hannibal faced a force of 50,000 Romans. He drew up his army with his best soldiers on the flanks. He attacked with his centre to engage the Romans and then his centre retreated. The Romans followed into the centre of Hannibal's crescent whereupon he commanded his flanks to close in on the Roman army most of whom were killed or captured. It is regarded as one of the greatest tactical feats in military history and is taught in officer training schools around the world.

Nelson at Trafalgar

On 21 October 1805, off the coast of Cadiz in Spain, the French and Spanish fleets, of 33 ships, were intercepted by a British fleet of 27 vessels under Admiral Nelson. The ensuing battle of Trafalgar was to determine the balance of power on the high seas and across Europe for the next century. In those times naval battles were fought by two opposing fleets which lined up in parallel and fired canon at each other. The vessels were called 'ships of the line' for this reason. However, in this battle Nelson employed a new tactic. He turned his ships through 90 degrees, organized them in two lines and sailed straight into the French and Spanish lines. The British ships presented a smaller target to enemy fire as they approached but they could not fire back. However, once they broke through the line they could fire devastating broadsides at close range.

This innovative approach worked brilliantly and gave Nelson his greatest triumph. Seventeen Franco-Spanish ships were captured or destroyed. The British lost no ships, but their victory was marred by the death of Lord Nelson, who was shot by a French marksman.

The greatest bluff of WW2

At the outbreak of the war, the German heavy cruiser *Admiral Graf Spee* was highly destructive, sinking nine merchant ships in the South Atlantic between September and December 1939. This formidable, armoured ship had six 28 cm guns and a top speed of 28 knots which meant that very few ships of the British or French navies could catch her. It was commanded by Captain Hans Langsdorff who had been awarded the Iron Cross for his actions as a lieutenant in the German navy in the First World War.

The British sent three light cruisers to intercept the *Admiral Graf Spee* and they engaged her in the Battle of the River Plate on 13 December 1939. The German ship inflicted heavy damage on the British ships, but it too was damaged and retreated under a smokescreen into the port of Montevideo in Uruguay.

While the *Admiral Graf Spee* was moored in Montevideo for repairs, British naval intelligence worked to convince the Germans that a vastly superior force was concentrating out-side Uruguayan waters to destroy the ship, if it attempted to break out of the harbour. The Admiralty broadcast a series of signals, on frequencies known to be intercepted by German intelligence. Such reports were also leaked to the press in South America. In reality the closest heavy units – the carrier Ark Royal and battlecruiser Renown – were over 2,500 miles away, much too far to intervene. Believing the British reports, Langsdorff discussed his options with his commanders in Berlin. His choices were either to break out and seek refuge in Buenos Aires, where the Argentine Government (which was sympathetic to Germany) would intern the ship, or to scuttle the ship in the Plate estuary.

Langsdorff was under instructions from Berlin not to let his ship fall into enemy hands and he was unwilling to risk the lives of his crew, so he decided to scuttle the ship. This took place on 18 December. The British had bluffed the Germans out of one of their most potent weapons. Langsdorff may have realized his mistake. On 20 December, he shot himself.

The Maginot Line

After their experiences in the First World War the British and French Military Commands assumed that any new war with Germany would be similar – a massive static engagement between two huge armies. So the French built massive defensive fortifications along the Maginot Line, named after the French Minister of War, André Maginot. It ran along the entire French border with Italy, Switzerland, Germany and Luxembourg. It did not extend to the English Channel as it was assumed that Belgium could be defended. The Maginot Line was designed to resist attacks by aerial bombardment, artillery and ground forces. The strategy was that the Maginot Line would blunt any invasion and allow time for mobilization and counterattack by allied forces.

However, when the Germans attacked in 1940 they did some lateral thinking. They discarded the tactics of the previous conflict and came up with a new kind of war, blitzkrieg. It involved fast-moving armoured divisions led by concentrations of tanks. They also used paratroopers and gliders. They invaded through the Low Countries, bypassing the Line to the north. The French and British had anticipated this and placed strong armies along the Belgian border.

There was a fatal weakness in the Allied plan. The Ardennes forest was lightly defended because it was assumed that this rough terrain would be unsuitable for tank attack. The Germans, aware of this flaw, advanced rapidly through the forest and across the river Meuse. They encircled and cut off the British and French forces in the north. The Allies were forced to retreat to Dunkirk where they were evacuated. The Maginot line was side-stepped, and France was defeated in a matter of weeks.

9/11

On 11 September 2001 the militant Islamic extremist network al-Qaida committed four coordinated suicide terrorist attacks against the United States. Nineteen terrorists hijacked four commercial airliners with the intention to crash the planes into prominent American buildings, inflicting mass casualties. They successfully crashed two planes into the North and South Towers of the World Trade Center in New York City causing the towers to collapse. A third plane crashed into the Pentagon building. The four crashed into a field after a passenger revolt stopped the planned attack.

The attacks resulted in 2,977 deaths and constituted the deadliest terrorist event in human history and the single deadliest incident for firefighters and law enforcement officers in the history of the US, with 412 killed. These outrages were masterminded by Osama Bin Laden who achieved his goal of mass casualties and damage on the US while gaining worldwide publicity for al-Qaida and its aims. The key unexpected lateral idea was the coordinated use of passenger planes loaded with fuel as weapons to be flown into buildings. Unfortunately, lateral thinking can be used by criminals and terrorists to make their work even more deadly.

13

Protect the parts that are not showing hits

Abraham Wald was born in 1902 in Transylvania which was part of Austria-Hungary and is now in Romania. His family were devout Jews who would not allow the boy to attend school on Saturdays, so he was home-schooled by his parents.

He was a brilliant mathematics student and he graduated with a PhD from the University of Vienna in 1931. However, because of discrimination against Jews it was very difficult for him to gain employment.

When the Nazis invaded Austria in 1938, Wald managed to emigrate to the US where he joined the Statistical Research Group at Columbia University. He was now able to bring his formidable skills in mathematics and operational research to military problems.

One challenge involved examining the distribution of damage from German fire on aircraft – in particular bombers. Extra protecting armour could be added to the plane but the more armour that was added the more weight that was carried. Certain parts of the fuselages appeared to receive more hits from anti-aircraft fire. The natural response from the military chiefs was to add more armour to these sections. Wald challenged this notion. He reasoned that enemy fire would be evenly distributed across the aircraft. He also observed that the sample contained only those aircraft which had survived the mission and returned. Consequently, the holes in the returning aircraft showed the areas where the plane could sustain damage and survive. Wald proposed that the Air Force reinforce the areas where the returning aircraft showed no damage as those were the areas where damage was lethal for the plane. He said, 'Protect the areas that are not showing hits.'

His insights proved correct and the story is renowned as an example of counter-intuitive thinking. It also illustrates the dangers of 'survivorship bias'.

After the war in 1950, Wald was invited to give a lecture tour in India. Sadly, while there he and his wife were killed in a plane crash.

14
Lateral thinking in architecture

Architecture involves a marriage between art and engineering so there is plenty of scope for lateral thinking. There are many examples both at the level of an individual construction building or in an innovation that affected many subsequent buildings. Here are some of my favourites.

The Great Pyramid at Giza, 2600 BC

This monumental construction was one of the seven wonders of the ancient world and the only one remaining intact to this day. It was a work of enormous ambition and needed around 15,000 people to labour over 10 years. It used some 5.5 million tonnes of limestone. It remained the largest and tallest building in the world for 3,800 years.

The arch, 2000 BC

The arch is a fine example of lateral thinking in action. Many ancient civilizations including the Egyptians, the Incas and (to a very large extent) the Greeks did not know of the arch or use it. They used an obvious and straightforward way to build their buildings with columns and lintels. The arch is first found in Mesopotamia around 2000 BC. It replaces tensile stress with compressive stress thus allowing for larger open spaces. It was used extensively by the Romans as seen in their aqueducts and temples.

The flying buttress, France, 12th century

As buildings grew larger with vaulted ceilings there was a need to protect the supporting walls from forces which pushed them outwards. A buttress can do this, and the flying buttress is more beautiful, lighter and more cost-effective than a conventional buttress. Although earlier examples can be found, the flying buttress really came into its own with the great Gothic French cathedrals built from the 12th century onwards. A fine early example is Notre Dame in Paris built in 1180. The flying buttress idea enabled bigger buildings with lighter walls and large windows.

St Basil's Cathedral, Moscow, 1551

This icon of Russia was built on the orders of Ivan the Terrible between 1551 and 1555. The cathedral has nine domes which are shaped like the flames of a bonfire. In *Russian Architecture and the West*, Dmitry Shvidkovsky says, 'It is like no other Russian building. Nothing similar can be found in the entire millennium of Byzantine tradition from the fifth to the fifteenth century… a strangeness that astonishes by its unexpectedness, complexity and dazzling interleaving of the manifold details of its design.'[13]

The Home Insurance Building, Chicago, 1885

This was the world's first skyscraper. It was designed by William Jenney in 1884 and completed the next year. In 1891 two additional floors were added to make a total of 12 floors, an unparalleled height at the time. It was the first tall building to be supported by a structural steel frame. It was opened in 1885 and demolished 46 years later in 1931.

The Eiffel Tower, Paris, 1889

This was the first building of its type and is still the highest wrought-iron building in the world. It was designed by Gustave Eiffel for the World's Fair in 1889 which celebrated the centenary of the French Revolution. It was highly controversial at the time and opposed by many powerful and influential people, so Eiffel suggested that it was a temporary structure which could be taken down after the Fair. It was the tallest man-made structure in the world and became massively popular. It is now the most visited paid monument in the world.

La Sagrada Familia, Barcelona, 1882 onwards

The Basilica of the Holy Family was designed by the Catalan architect Antoni Gaudi. It was started in 1882 and has yet to be completed. It combines Gothic and Art Nouveau styles. The art critic Rainer Zerbst said, 'It is probably impossible to find a church building anything like it in the entire history of art.' Architecture critic Paul Goldberger described it as 'the most extraordinary personal interpretation of Gothic architecture since the Middle Ages'.

Sydney Opera House, 1973

The Sydney Opera House is widely regarded as one of the world's most distinctive buildings and a masterpiece of 20th-century architecture. This expressionist design by

Danish architect Jorn Utzon won an international contest with over 200 entries. It went on to win architecture's highest honour, the Pritzker Prize. The design included pre-cast concrete shells and the idea was based on the sails of a ship.

Lloyd's Building, London, 1986

The Lloyd's building, designed by Richard Rogers, has a ground-breaking feature, 'Bowellism': all the services for the building, such as ducts and elevators, are located on the outside in order to maximize space inside. It has been called the inside-out building.

Gate Tower Building, Osaka, 1992

This 16-storey office block is remarkable because it has a four-lane highway running right through the building. Floors five to seven are unoccupied because the motorway bridge crosses through the building there.

Guggenheim Museum, Bilbao, 1997

Architect Frank Gehry designed a highly innovative building with monumental shapes in titanium and glass. It has become one of the most admired works of contemporary architecture.

Bird's Nest Stadium, Beijing, 2007

The Chinese National Stadium, which has a capacity of 80,000, is known as the Bird's Nest. It was designed by Swiss architects Jacques Herzog and Pierre de Meuron with help from Chinese artist Ai Weiwei and architect Li Xinggang.

The design was based on Chinese ceramics and features a criss-cross of random-looking steel strips that resemble a bird's nest.

Much of architecture is of an everyday, utilitarian and mundane nature but there are still opportunities for architects to produce brilliant new concepts if the project owners are brave enough to give them the freedom and budget to do so.

15

When something unexpected happens, get curious

We often treat an unexpected or surprising happening as an irritation or distraction. It delays us from getting on with the job, so we quickly work around it. But sometimes it pays to step back and ponder the meaning of what serendipity has just handed us. Consider these unexpected occurrences.

1 In New York in 1908 a tea merchant sent customers samples of tea leaves in small silken sachets for them to try. Customers were supposed to empty out the contents but instead some put the whole silk bag into the teapot and then added hot water.

2 In 1928 a Scottish bacteriologist returned from his vacation to find that one of his Petri dishes had a strange mould growing in it.

3 In the early 1940s a Swiss engineer went for a walk with his dog in the Jura mountains. When he came home, he saw that his trousers and the dog's fur contained many tiny seed burrs.

4 In 1946 an engineer at Raytheon discovered that a sweet in his pocket melted when he worked near an active radar tube.

5 In the 1970s a technician working for a music accessory company wired a circuit incorrectly. The component made a weird moaning sound.

6 In 1989 a pharmaceutical company ran a clinical trial on an experimental drug which was designed to treat heart-related chest pains. It was not particularly effective in that regard but men on the trial reported an unusual side-effect.

Each of these incidents could have been treated as an annoying accident. Most people might have ignored the customers, cleaned the Petri dishes, brushed off their trousers, removed the sticky sweet or rewired the circuit correctly. Fortunately for us the protagonists in these stories all welcomed the unexpected event, investigated and then acted.

1 When Thomas Sullivan heard that customers were happy with this new arrangement, he designed small containers for large-scale production. He created the teabag. He made bags of gauze and then paper. He later added string and a tag so the bag could be easily removed. Incidentally, according to the *Daily Mirror* a survey by English Heritage showed that people rated the teabag as one of the most important inventions of all time, alongside the wheel and the internet.

2 Sir Alexander Fleming saw that the mould had rejected the bacteria in the dish. He had discovered penicillin – almost by accident. It was a piece of good fortune that led to the development of antibiotics and the saving of millions of lives.

3 George de Mestral examined the burrs under a microscope and saw that they had tiny hooks which caught in the trouser fabric. He went on to develop a new way to fasten materials – Velcro. The word comes from the French words *velours* and *crochet* – a velvet hook.

4 Percy Spencer developed the world's first microwave oven because of this accident.

5 Scott Burnham adapted the strange wail into a guitar-pedal sound. He invented the Rat, a pedal that thousands of bands from Nirvana to Radiohead used to enhance their music.

6 Pfizer had stumbled on to Viagra.

In his book *Inventology*, Pagan Kennedy claims that almost half of all inventions started with a serendipitous process.[14] Often this was the result of ideas or discoveries that people had while working on something else.

Kennedy goes on to say that inventors are often polymath connectors 'who by luck or design are able to bring together knowledge from several fields'. She points out that the people most likely to solve problems on the Innocentive crowd-sourcing site are outsiders to the field of the problem.

When something unexpected happens don't get annoyed – get curious. Find out why. The customer with a weird complaint or a weird use for your product is one hundred times more interesting than the customer who is happy using your product in a conventional way. Welcome the surprising. Lateral thinkers are open-minded and quick to learn from accidents. They are ready to observe and adapt when the unexpected happens.

Part Three
Lateral thinking tools and everyday hacks

16
How to use the Six Thinking Hats

The Six Thinking Hats is a method developed by Edward de Bono.[15] It is highly effective as a discipline for holding discussions, running meetings and making decisions. It involves some lateral thinking as it deliberately displaces you from your usual thinking approach. However, it is more accurately described as a parallel thinking technique because it encourages all members of a group to think in the same style at the same time. It allows the team to review issues in a much more rounded and effective way. It has been used in board rooms, in social clubs, in jury rooms and in many other kinds of group meetings.

Conventional meetings often involve adversarial thinking. This style of thinking is commonplace, and it comes to us from the Greeks. One person advances a thesis, and another person will criticize it and maybe propose an antithesis. This is well illustrated in a court of law where the prosecution will present a strong case that the accused is guilty, and the defence lawyer will try to rebut all the prosecutions arguments and then propose that the defendant is innocent. Similarly in the UK Parliament the Government spokesperson will tell us what a great job the government is doing and how effective its policies are. The opposition parties have a duty to oppose so they argue that the government's ideas and approaches are wrong. It is what de Bono called 'I am right, you are wrong' thinking. Part of the problem with this approach is that ego can impede judgement. Once you have adamantly advanced your case it is hard to back down and admit that the other side has a point. No one likes to lose face, so people tend to dig harder into their initial positions.

Another problem with conventional business meetings is that the most senior or most powerful person in the room will often start the meeting and state a point of view. People with lower status are then reluctant to challenge this view.

The six hats method overcomes the problems of adversarial thinking by getting people to think in parallel using six different hats to denote six different styles of thinking. We all wear the same colour hat at the same time, and this shapes the meeting.

Let's say we have a meeting to review a certain proposition. We start with the white hat. This is the hat of information or data. What are the facts that we know about the situation? We review the facts, statistics and analyses without passing any opinions or drawing any conclusions. Sometimes we will have a white paper containing such data circulated before the meeting. While wearing the white hat we might identify new data that needs to be gathered.

We take off our white hats and don the red hats. The red hat is the hat of feelings and emotions. This is an interesting hat because normally in meetings we do not talk about our feelings, but feelings are important. While wearing this hat we ask everyone to express their feelings about this proposal. People must say what they feel in terms of an emotion – from their hearts rather than their heads. So, they cannot say something like 'The return on investment will be poor.' They should state a feeling, e.g. 'I feel angry about this.' Or 'I feel excited.' Or 'I feel nervous.' No one can argue with these statements. If you feel angry, then you feel angry. The feelings are recorded, and I like to list them as negative feelings on one column, positive feelings on another and neutral feelings in a third.

We now move on to the yellow hat which is the hat of sunshine and optimism. With this hat on, we all have to say what is good about this idea. What would the benefits be if it worked well? Even if you think this is a terrible idea and it comes from your worst enemy in the company, you have to find something positive to say about it. We list as many positives as we can and then we prioritize them. What are the biggest advantages of this idea? Everyone has to stay positive and optimistic while wearing the yellow hat.

Next, we move to the black hat which is the hat of pessimism, of risk, of caution. Everyone must find fault with the idea. So even if you think it is a terrific idea you have to identify some potential risks or downsides. Cynics who generally wear a black hat at work were pushed out of their comfort zone with the yellow hat and optimists who think every promising idea should be implemented are now forced to think differently. Once we have a good list of black hat drawbacks and disadvantages, we prioritize to identify the most serious issues.

Before we move on it is worthwhile to summarize what has happened so far. We have worn four hats and adopted four thinking styles. In doing so we have reviewed the key facts, summarized everyone's initial feelings, listed and prioritized the advantages of the proposal and we have listed and prioritized the disadvantages of the proposal. We have made tremendous progress but we have not had an argument yet. There has been no scope in the process for an argument.

Of course, we have to have an open discussion on the proposal but this happens while we wear the next hat – the green hat.

The green hat is the hat of growth, creativity and ideas. While wearing this hat we are looking for ways to improve the proposal. The sort of question we might ask is, 'Can we find a way to deliver the benefits of the proposal while mitigating the risks and downsides?' People make suggestions and explore each other's ideas. After this discussion the group will generally try to reach a decision while still wearing the green hat. There are three main possibilities: to accept the proposal as is, to reject the proposal or to accept an amended proposal which contains some of the ideas generated with the green hat. If there is a substantially different proposition we may need to go back to the white, red, yellow or black hats.

There is one final hat, the blue hat. This is the hat of process or control. We might put it on at the beginning to plan the six hat process. We might put it on at the end to review how the process worked. Someone can put it on in the middle and point out that the process is not being followed – 'You are wearing a black hat and criticizing while we should all be wearing the yellow hat.'

I have run many meetings using the six hats method and canvassed people's views afterwards. How did this meeting compare to a normal business meeting? People are generally enthusiastic and say that the hats delivered a meeting which was much quicker, more focused and more effective. They looked at the proposal from different points of view and no one voice dominated. It leads to better decisions and those decision have more buy-in from the participants.

17
The Disney Method for creative ideas

People complain about meetings. There are too many, they are poorly managed, they overrun, there is groupthink (as we have seen in Chapter 3) where people agree too much, there are dominant individuals who rule the conversation, there is little creativity, there are few decisions made. The list of complaints is long, and usually justified. One of the best ways of overcoming these difficulties is to use de Bono's Six Thinking Hats but another and less well-known approach is the Disney Method. It is so called because supposedly Walt Disney used it with his creative teams. It is particularly effective when developing and reviewing innovative solutions and projects. The method is a parallel thinking technique as it involves four different mindsets, and everyone adopts the same mindset approach when in one of the four phases of the meeting. After each phase the group leaves the room and then re-enters with a different mindset. The physical act of leaving and coming back helps to reinforce the change in attitude.

You assemble a small group of people with diverse experiences and skills. Then you articulate the challenge. The problem or objective is clearly described. Initially the group thinks as outsiders and people review the facts, data and external viewpoints regarding the issue at hand. They might take the roles of consultants, customers, suppliers or competitors in order to get a more rounded view of the issue. Notes are written up on flip charts or captured on a computer.

The group then leaves the room and re-enters, but this time as dreamers. They strive to imagine an ideal solution without any constraints. They brainstorm all sorts of ideas to resolve the problem using divergent thinking. No criticism or judgment is allowed. Many ideas are generated and written down. There are no limits on the ideas and people are encouraged to imagine wonderful solutions without being concerned about resources or approvals.

The group leaves the room and then returns as realizers. They are now solid realists with a practical, constructive mindset. They review the ideas that the dreamers generated and apply criteria to converge on the best ideas. Once they have selected the best idea, they work it up into a mini project plan. They detail next steps, approvals, estimated costs and timescales. They also list the risks and benefits.

The group leaves and comes back using the fourth thinking style. Everyone becomes a critic who reviews the plan in order to identify problems, obstacles and risks. They are not negative in a cynical sense, but they are critical and constructive. Their objective is to spot the risks and issues with the plan and to make it better.

You can repeat any phase of the process as might be needed. If you now have a good plan with clearly identified risk and benefits you might consider the process complete. Or you might go back to the outsiders phase and consider how the plan will be viewed externally. If the critics liked the plan but came up with serious objections, then you might want to work as realizers on the details of the plan. If the objections cannot be overcome, you can go back to the dreamers' stage and create entirely new possibilities.

Some people find this method easier to use than the Six Thinking Hats. It is important for the facilitator of the group to keep people in their thinking roles at each stage. If it is well run the Disney Method is fun, energetic and creative. It will deliver good ideas and a well-considered project plan.

18
Use the three Greeks to improve your powers of persuasion

We often find ourselves in a position where we need to communicate ideas and influence other people. We might want to change their mind, to sell them on an idea or to secure their agreement to a proposal. How can you go about this? Should we just collect our best arguments and forcefully deliver them while batting away objections? Is there a better way, a smarter way, a lateral way?

A fruitful way to approach these situations is to use the three Greeks, ancient concepts that are proven to work. In my experience most people use only one of the three Greeks, and they would be much more effective if they used all three.

The three Greeks are Ethos, Pathos and Logos. Ethos refers to values and standing, authority and credibility. The word *ethics* derives from the Greek word *ethos*. Pathos in this context means feelings and emotions. The words *empathy* and *sympathy* are derived from the Greek word *pathos*. Logos means logic, reason and analysis. When we try to persuade people using facts, statistics, deduction and reasoning we are using logos.

How can you use all three Greeks to increase your effectiveness? Let's start with Ethos. Why should someone listen to you? What authority do you have? When you hear a speaker introduced at a conference there is often a short description given of the speaker's achievements and credentials – this establishes their ethos. It gives the audience a reason to listen and believe. If you are meeting someone for the first time it pays to establish your credentials and expertise – preferably before the meeting but otherwise early in the meeting. The trick is to do this without sounding as though you are boastful. In a preliminary email you might say something like 'I have worked in this field for seven years and have helped X and Y to successfully accomplish Z.' Or you might insert a link and say 'I thought you might possibly be interested to read this article I published on the subject.' The purpose is to establish some level of standing and authority before the meeting. If you are expert, it is important to communicate your expertise.

Pathos involves appealing to the feelings of the person or people you are meeting. If you listen to the speeches of Martin Luther King or to the pre-election addresses of Barack Obama, you will observe they appeal heavily to emotion. They paint a vision of a better future in which people can have hope and pride. These speeches were highly effective in changing people's minds. In everyday conversation and particularly in business, we tend to shun appeals to emotion, but people's feelings are powerful forces. If we can appeal to pride, excitement, altruism or hope then we can inspire people to change. We can also talk about fear, disappointment, anger and frustration as emotions that can be overcome.

The third Greek is the one that most of us use most of the time. We appeal to facts, rational arguments, logic and reason to advance our case. 'The reason we should do this is because it will save money and increase sales.' These might well be good arguments and we should certainly deploy logos to advance our cause. However, if we can first establish our credibility with ethos and then also appeal to pathos by painting a picture of a better future in which we can be happy and take pride then we are much more likely to persuade. If we can convince with logic and emotion then we will be doubly effective. Don't take just one Greek to your next meeting or presentation – take all three.

19
Where do innovative ideas come from?

Cities around the world suffer from a common problem – a shortage of affordable, decent-quality housing. Cutworks Studio, a design company based in Paris and Amsterdam, has developed an approach called PolyBlocs – modularly constructed residential sites consisting of individual block rooms which can be stacked in different ways to create an array of sizes and shapes. The basic component is called a PolyRoom which is shaped like a shipping container. They provide multi-functional spaces with flexible configurations that include a range of window and door placement options. Other features include a bed which can be folded upwards, tables with built-in cupboards and compact bathrooms. The PolyRooms are designed to be stacked like Lego bricks.

This is an innovative but derivative idea. Where might it have come from? Let's imagine we were working in the design studio trying to brainstorm ways to create affordable urban housing. We could have started in a number of places to come up with this idea.

Analyse the problem. It takes a lot of time and so costs a lot of money to have workers on site constructing a new building in a city centre. How can we minimize the build time? Could we build the building elsewhere and then quickly assemble it on site? How can we *minimize* the assembly time?

Go back in time. Let's think about prefab buildings – which have been around for a long time. In 1160 the Normans built a prefab castle! How can we update these old ideas to make them sustainable and suitable for modern needs?

Adapt a different kind of housing solution – mobile homes. Could we take the wheels off a mobile home and turn it into a stackable unit?

Start with a different industry. How does shipping make the best and most economical use of tight spaces? They use containers. Could we take the idea of a container and apply it to housing?

Let's play a game. What game involves fitting things together? Let's use Lego as a metaphor for building and see where that leads.

Rearrange the components or the process. We normally build a house sequentially starting with foundations and walls, then doors and windows and services, then finally fitments like beds and baths. Could we rearrange this sequence and put them together all at the same time?

Innovative ideas can come from myriad sources. There are many ways we could have approached this problem. A well-facilitated brainstorm using a technique such as SCAMPER or Similes would probably have thrown up this idea along with many others. We need lots of innovative ideas to solve today's problems. The more different starting points we use, the more likely we are to generate winning ideas.

20
The Six Serving Men

When presented with a problem it is tempting to rush in and suggest solutions. The more experienced, the more powerful, the more forceful you are, the greater the temptation to advance your immediate solutions. But if your understanding of the problem is incomplete or just plain wrong then you will often come up with a bad solution because it addresses the wrong problem. We have learnt from studies in quality and Six Sigma methods that root cause analysis gives a deeper understanding of fundamental issues and therefore a better chance of generating good solutions. There are many books on advanced root cause analysis methods. Here is a simple technique which can help you to quickly identify the basic causes of a problem

Six Serving Men is a team exercise that examines an issue from twelve different viewpoints. It can be used on your own or with a group. The lateral component is that it forces you to take different perspectives – twelve in all. It is based on a poem by Rudyard Kipling:

> I keep six honest serving-men
> (They taught me all I knew);
> Their names are What and Why and When
> And How and Where and Who.

Let's consider it as a workshop tool. We probe the topic using these questioning words from a positive and negative perspective. The issue is defined and then twelve sheets of flip chart paper are arranged around the room. On each sheet one of the twelve questions is written as the heading and the team splits up into small groups to come up with many answers to the question or questions they are given. Suppose the issue is, 'How can we improve customer service in our retail centres?' The questions could be constructed as follows:

1 What is good customer service?

2 What is not good customer service? (Or what is bad customer service?)

3 Why do we get good customer services?

4 Why do we get bad customer service?

5 When is there good customer service?

6 When is there bad customer service?

7 How do we get good customer service?

8 How do we get bad customer service?

9 Where is there good customer service?

10 Where is there bad customer service?

11 Who gives good customer service?

12 Who gives poor customer service?

By repeatedly approaching the questions of good service and bad service and by forcing people to come up with new answers and inputs a broad picture is painted of the issue and the underlying factors. The ideas on the sheets are analysed, prioritized and combined to give a deeper understanding of the problem and some insights as to why it is happening. These ideas then become the starting point for a plan to address the issue.

In meetings we tend to default to the questions, 'Why do we have this problem?' and 'What can we do about it?' But for anything other than simple problems these questions are premature. First we need to thoroughly understand the problem and the twelve different approaches work well. It is very important to apply each question literally. So 'Who gives good service?' might be answered with:

> Joan in the furniture department.
> More experienced staff.
> People who have the time.
> People who have the motivation.
> People who are interested in the customer.

'Who gives bad service?' might be answered:

New or inexperienced staff.

People who are too busy.

People who do not know the answers to the customers' questions.

Office staff who are filling in for sales staff on their break.

Similarly, for the 'when' questions. We want specific time of day, day of week or circumstance in which good or poor service is given.

We gather a large number of answers to the twelve questions and then prioritize the most insightful answers and share the results. Now we have a sound basis for a brainstorm to find ways to improve customer service. Each of the answers generated by the Six Serving Men will yield many ideas – some routine and some truly creative. Who knows? Perhaps we will select a plan to get Joan to run a training session for other members of staff!

21

Games that can boost the brain

Thinkers relish the challenge and stimulation of intellectual games. They enjoy games for the pure thrill of exercising their minds and judgements in pursuit of victory. You can take pleasure in any number of great games. There are many benefits in playing games and in adopting a playful approach to life in general. Games help develop a range of vital skills in children and they love playing them. Games can also develop the same skills in adults but many grown-ups consider games to be childish and not worthy of their time. This is a pity and a missed opportunity.

In 2022 Sam Wass, a child psychologist and neuroscientist at the University of East London, reported on his studies of children's brains as they play.[16] He found that there are more links between different neurons in a young child's brain than there are in an adult one, and as a result their brains are 'messier'. Play helps make sort things out. Wass says, 'You're making connections between different parts of the brain which haven't necessarily been connected before and then you're repeating it. It's through this process of repetition that you're helping to strengthen the connections between these different brain areas.'

The same report quoted Drew Altschul, a psychologist at the University of Edinburgh who had been following a study that had been tracking the development of children's behaviour in Scotland since the 1940s. The research studied how the thinking skills of people change as they grew older. He said the research suggests playing games can help preserve brain function: 'People who played more games at age 70 had a less steep decline overall in their thinking skills.'

Which games should we play? It appears that all games using the brain help the brain. But let's focus now on imagination and lateral thinking. Here are my favourite games for developing creativity.

1 *Charades*. Your grandparents probably played this venerable parlour game. It requires no equipment but plenty of imagination, improvisation and lateral thinking. And it is often hilarious fun.

2 *Pictionary*. Similar to Charades but now with a graphical theme. Can you draw pictures which convey useful clues?

3 *Cryptic crosswords*. A good cryptic crossword clue is devilishly cunning. You have to stretch your mind in all sorts of ingenious ways to figure out what it means.

4 *Lateral thinking puzzles*. These are strange situations where you have to ask many questions, test your assumptions and come at the problem from different directions. Great for all the family on a long car journey.

5 *Code Names*. A great game for four people which tests your ability to think of clues that give clever connections between multiple words.

6 *Dingbats*. Dingbats are rebuses or visual word puzzles where you have to figure out the common phrase or word represented by what you see. The advice is to say what you see – but can you look laterally enough to see the answer?

7 *Escape rooms.* Often involve ingenious clues and puzzles which you have to solve to move from one room to the next.

8 *Rory's Story Cubes.* A set of nine dice with different images create random stimuli. They fire your imagination with multiple starting points for storytelling.

Here are some of my favourite games for developing logic, reasoning and memory.

1 *Chess.* The king of games. It represents a pure cerebral struggle between two minds. It teaches strategy, tactics, positional play and the benefits of absolute concentration. Every home should have a set. Every child should learn to play. Everyone can enjoy the challenge.

2 *Sudoku* is good for concentration, deduction and detailed numerical analysis

3 *Scrabble.* The classic word game. You have to make the most of whatever letter tiles are in your hand using the available tiles on the board. Skilled players see remarkable possibilities and know a range of obscure and short words that they use adroitly.

4 *Monopoly.* This is the game that Fidel Castro banned when he came to power in Cuba because he saw it as a model for capitalism. There is a large element of luck but the skilled player will often triumph because they focus on the right resources and develop a set quickly. It teaches trading skills and probabilities.

5 *Bridge.* There are many great card games but surely the finest is bridge. The bidding and the play of the cards represent two different skill sets, with the play having amazing subtleties. Good players remember all the cards played and can quickly deduce the lie of the hidden cards. Most players learn whist first before graduating to bridge.

6 *Cluedo* (Clue in the US). This is a popular family game which is great fun. Can you put the clues together and figure out who is the murderer?

7 *Backgammon*. An excellent game for two players with its own mixture of luck, skill and gambling. You can choose risky or cagey strategies and double the value of game on occasions.

8 *Poker*. Some people wrongly think that poker is all about bluffing. It is a highly demanding intellectual exercise in which the skilful players read their opponents. You need nerves of steel and excellent understanding of the probabilities to succeed. This is a costly game to learn and it can be dangerous but surely it is one of life's greatest pastimes.

9 *Trivial Pursuit*. The parent of all quiz games. This will test your general knowledge and your ability to think in the same clever ways as the puzzle-setters.

10 *Video games and apps* can boost reaction times and dexterity. They are immensely popular with children and young adults and can become addictive.

22
Riddles to make you think laterally

What does a dog do that a man steps into? There is an obvious answer to this riddle but of course it is not the answer we are looking for. To find the solution you have to sidestep the obvious and discover something else that a dog does and that a man steps into. The answer is pants. This is clever play on words because 'pants' is a verb when a dog does it but a noun when a man steps into them.

Good riddles are cunning trick questions that sucker you into the wrong answer. You have to think laterally to crack them. Here are twelve of my favourites. How many can you get right? (Only those that you have not seen before count in your score!)

1 In your estimation how many bricks does it take to complete the average detached brick house in England?

2 In what month do plumbers eat the least?

3 If it took 10 people 8 hours to build a wall how long would it take 5 people to build it?

4 Why do the Chinese eat more rice than Japanese people?

5 A Muslim bricklayer living in England cannot be buried on Church ground even if they convert to Christianity. Why not?

6 Removing an appendix is called an appendectomy, removing tonsils is called a tonsillectomy. What is it called when they remove a growth from your head?

7 Why are US soldiers not to have rifles any longer?

8 What three things that you can eat can you never have for breakfast?

9 How can you drop a raw egg on to a concrete floor without cracking it?

10 What is the last thing you take off before going to bed at night?

11 In your estimation how many seconds are there in a year?

12 If an atheist died in a church, what would they put on his coffin?

Take your time. Watch out for red herrings, misleading directions and cunning tricks. Then check your answers on page 227.

23
The Random Word method

I facilitate creative thinking sessions for corporate customers and it is sometimes a challenge to displace the delegates out of their conventional ways of thinking. If I want to generate really creative and unorthodox ideas, then I often introduce a random stimulus. The easiest one to start with is the Random Word.

Just pick up a dictionary and choose a noun at random. Write the word on the top of the flip chart paper and then underneath list five or six attributes of that word. Then force connections between the word or its attributes and the problem to be solved. You will find that all sorts of new associations spring to mind.

Say the problem is how to attract the best applicants to join your company. The random word from the dictionary is: eucalyptus. You write eucalyptus on the sheet and then list some attributes or associations – say Australia, gum, Koala bear, branches, medicine. Some of the ideas that might be triggered are:

- Recruit Australians and New Zealanders.
- Offer the opportunity to take time off and travel the world.
- Offer free packs of dental gum to anyone who applies.

- Stick notices about your job opportunities on boards at gyms and clubs.

- Run a recruitment seminar at a zoo.

- Give applicants a branded teddy bear to show what a caring company you are.

- Offer medical insurance and health checks.

- Run a publicity event that helps a local hospital.

- Show people how their career can branch out if they join your company.

Keep adding suggestions until you run out or ideas and then turn over the flip chart and pick a new random noun from the dictionary. Some words work much better than others though you never know which until you try them. I generally find that simple concrete nouns like fish, corner, stick or house work better than abstract nouns like faith or sorrow. But you have to try with whatever you get. When you have a long list of ideas from several random words then you evaluate them using some agreed criteria to select and refine the best ones.

Why does a stimulus like the random word work? It forces the brain to start from a new departure point, to come at the problem from a new direction. The brain is a lazy organ; it will automatically lapse into familiar patterns and solve problems the way it has always done unless you give it a jog and start it from a new point. However, the brain is clever at forcing connections between disparate things so when you prompt your mind with a strange stimulus it responds by finding creative connections.

You can also use random pictures, objects, songs or a walk to introduce brainstorm stimuli. You can bring along a selection of photos of random objects or ask people to bring an object that they think will be unusual (without telling them why). You can also ask people to go for a walk in a city centre or around an art gallery or museum and then tell you about something they saw. That then becomes the starting point for the brainstorm.

This method works well with groups, but you can also use it when working on your own. Write down the challenge. Then pick up the dictionary and off you go. Try it – you will probably be surprised by the results.

24
Similes displace your thinking

How can you get people in your brainstorm meeting to think differently? A solid lateral technique is called Similes (sometimes knows as 51 Miles).

Gather your group. You state the challenge and then get everyone to write down on their own sheet of paper: 'Our problem is like…' Each person working alone then completes the sentence. They can make several suggestions. They must do this in silence so that they are not influenced by each other's ideas. You are looking to find a broadly similar challenge in a completely different field. If, for example, your problem is in business then you would ask who has had a problem like this in warfare, sport, entertainment, transport, history, politics, education, health, research, music etc.

The likenesses do not have to be accurate – they are feelings rather than exact analogies, but each can act as a trigger. You share the similes and write them on a flip chart. The group chooses one that they think is a good analogy for the initial challenge. You brainstorm the chosen simile to find solutions for that problem. Participants have to think as though they are in that environment. You then analyse the ideas to see if any will translate to the original problem and give a working solution there.

Let me give you an example of this in action. I ran a workshop for a group of newspaper advertising managers and one of the challenges we had was 'How can we reduce absenteeism?' Many of the telephone sales people would take days off in this high-pressure job. We asked everyone to find a simile for this problem of absenteeism. Here are some of the suggestions we were given as to what the problem is like:

'… getting a child to brush his teeth'

'… persuading undergraduates to go to lectures'

'… sticking to a diet'

'… getting the third football team to all show up for the match on Saturday'

'… getting teenagers to clean their rooms'

'… making motorists observe speed limits'

The group chose the football team simile, and we brainstormed that situation. How can you get the football team to all show up for a match? Several of the ideas we came up with involved peer pressure. We then translated each idea to see if it had any applications in the original context, a newspaper advertising sales office. We ended up with a group bonus for attendance with published tables of who had been absent so far each month. The resulting peer pressure cut absenteeism significantly. Getting a good working simile is the key to this exercise. The good news is that you only need one good simile from all those contributed by the group. Having said that, if you have time you can try more than one of the similes to brainstorm and translate. Each analogy draws on different personal experiences and each will give a different perspective and set of ideas when used in a brainstorm.

25
Roll the Dice

The use of chance is a key element in lateral thinking. How can you deliberately introduce chance into your creative thinking? The Random Word method is highly effective. Here is another brainstorm method for you to try – Roll the Dice.

It works well with groups of four to six people and is excellent for forcing unusual combinations of ideas and settings. If you have more people, you can divide into competing teams in separate rooms. The only equipment needed is a flip chart and a dice.

You select a challenge and then identify three or four characteristics and list six choices for each. For example, say you wanted to create a new TV drama you might choose the parameters set out in the table below.

	Lead character	Secondary character	Crime	Location
1	Detective	Vagrant	Murder	Hospital
2	Politician	Postal worker	Robbery	School
3	Priest	Shop worker	Blackmail	TV station
4	Company CEO	Teenager	Kidnapping	Football club
5	Doctor	Journalist	Fraud	Restaurant
6	Teacher	Window cleaner	Smuggling	Theatre

You then roll the dice four times. Say you roll 4, 4, 2, 6. The team has to conceive and design a plan for a TV programme about a CEO and a teenager who get involved in a robbery at a theatre. You could spin a coin to determine the genders of the two main characters.

The team spends 10 minutes discussing how this could work. They might then roll the dice again to get another combination and see what they can make of it. There are 1,296 different possible combinations! After three or four goes they select the most promising idea, put together a plan and present it to the other teams and the moderator.

I have found that this method can work well for new product, service and marketing initiatives. This approach forces you to review combinations that you would not normally consider. It is quite remarkable how combinations that initially look unattractive can be moulded into interesting propositions.

26
Lateral thinking puzzles

Lateral thinking puzzles are a form of mental exercise game. They are strange situations often drawn from real life. You are given a limited amount of information and have to find out what is going on. Each has a perfectly good explanation – you have to find it. The puzzles are not designed to be solved by the individual reading them. They work best when played as a game in a pair or a group. One person knows the solution and others ask closed questions, to which they receive the answers, 'yes', 'no' or 'irrelevant'. The puzzles test how well you can check your assumptions, how well you can question and your ability to approach the problem from different angles. You have to put together various pieces of information, think logically and think laterally. When you get stuck they can be frustrating – but that is part of the process and the process should be fun. The answers are on page 228.

Mountains ahead

You are seated next to the pilot of a small plane at an altitude of one mile. Huge mountains loom directly ahead. The pilot does not change speed, direction or elevation, yet you survive. How come?

The key

Every night before she went to bed a woman carefully locked all the doors of her house. Then she placed the front door key inside a bucket of cold water. In the morning she retrieved the key from the bucket in order to open the door. Why did she put the key in the water?

The damaged car

A man was the proud owner of a beautiful and expensive Mercedes sports car. One day he drove it to a multi-storey car park and then smashed the windows, scratched the doors and ripped out the radio. Why?

The blanket mystery

A man walked up a hill carrying a blanket. Because of this 100 people died. How?

The seven-year itch

While digging a garden, a woman unearthed a large metal box filled with money and jewellery. For seven years she spent none of the money and told no one what she had found. Then she suddenly bought a new house, a new car and a fur coat. How come?

Sand trap

Why did a man go to great trouble to bury in the desert 15 brand new Mercedes Benz cars greased and wrapped in plastic?

These puzzles are drawn from *Great Lateral Thinking Puzzles* by Paul Sloane and Des MacHale.[17]

27
Go for quantity of ideas

Linus Pauling was a brilliant scientist who won two Nobel prizes in different fields. He said, 'The way to get good ideas is to get lots of ideas and throw the bad ones away.'

Most managers like to be seen as decisive. They can quickly come up with an idea for tackling a problem. Doing something is generally (but not always) a better option that doing nothing. But the first answer we come up with is unlikely to be the best one.

A better approach is to take a little time to generate a long list of possible ideas and then evaluate them in order to select one or more to try. Our first idea is often the most obvious, the most straightforward response. It is rarely the best response. As we mull over the problem and force more and more possible solutions, we generate less conventional, less routine, less automatic choices – we come up with the creative, the radical and the better options.

One of the problems with the Western education system is that it teaches that for most questions there is one correct answer. Examinations with multiple-choice questions force the student to try to select the right answer and avoid the wrong ones. So when our students leave school they are steeped in a system that says find the 'right answer' and you have solved the problem. The real world is not like that. For almost every problem there are multiple solutions. We have to unlearn the school approach and instead adopt an attitude of always looking for more and better answers.

To be really creative you need to generate a large number of ideas before you refine the process down to a few to test out. To make your organization more innovative you have to increase the yield. Why do you need more ideas? Because when you start generating ideas you generate the obvious, easy answers. As you come up with more and more ideas you produce more wacky, crazy, creative ideas – the kind that can lead to really radical solutions.

The management guru Gary Hamel talks about 'corporate sperm count' – the virility test of how many ideas your business generates.[18] Many managers fear that too many ideas will be unmanageable but the most innovative companies revel in multitudes of ideas.

When BMW launched its Virtual Innovation Agency (VIA) to canvass suggestions from people all round the world it received 4,000 ideas in the first week. The Toyota Corporation in-house suggestion scheme generates some two million ideas a year. Even more remarkably, over 90 per cent of the suggestions are implemented. Quantity works.

Thomas Edison was prolific in his experiments. His development of the electric light took over 9,000 experiments and that of the storage cell around 50,000. He still holds the record for the most patents – over 1,090 in his name. After his death 3,500 notebooks full of his ideas and jottings were found. It was the prodigiousness of his output that led to so many breakthroughs. Picasso painted over 20,000 works. Bach composed at least one work a week. The great geniuses produced quantity as well as quality. Sometimes it is only by producing the many that we can produce the great.

When you start brainstorming or using other creative techniques the best idea might not come in the first 20 or the first 100 ideas. The quality of ideas does not degrade with quantity – often the later ideas are the more radical ones from which a truly lateral solution can be developed.

Part Four
Practical tips and everyday hacks

28
Force yourself to think outside the box

We think inside frameworks of assumptions and conventions. We think in patterns and ways that are comfortable for us. We think in ways that reinforce our view of the world. How can we force ourselves to think differently? Here is a brief checklist of suggestions, many of which are covered in more detail in this book.

1 First, recognize that we all live inside boxes which frame our view of the world. We are constrained by our assumptions.

2 Stay curious and open-minded. Ask many questions about any situation and be receptive to different points of view.

3 List the underlying ground rules and assumptions. Then for each one ask this question: 'What if the opposite were true?' Wherever you see a rule ask, 'What would happen if this rule were broken?'

4 Use some lateral thinking techniques to brainstorm wild ideas – e.g. Similes or the Random Word method.

5 Discuss the situation with a complete outsider. For instance, ask an army officer, a child, a priest, a doctor, a car mechanic, an artist, a comedian, a musician, a criminal or a detective. Note how they ask different types of questions.

6 Deliberately read periodicals and visit websites that disagree with your point of view in order to be aware of different perspectives.

7 Don't accept theories and models at face value. Test ideas in a small way in the real world. Place more trust in empirical results.

8 Find out how people from different countries and cultures view the situation.

9 When someone criticizes you or disagrees with you, do not dismiss or reject them. Say to yourself, 'There might be something valuable in what they say.'

10 Mix with people you do not normally mix with. Mix with people who are unlike you in background and attitude. Ask their opinions.

11 Enrol in courses in unconnected disciplines. Take online and classroom courses in fields which interest you but are remote from your current skills.

12 Visit museums, art galleries and libraries.

13 Dip into a different culture by watching foreign-language films with subtitles.

14 Introduce the random. Read the daily random article on Wikipedia. Take non-fiction books at random from the library or second-hand bookshops.

15 Stop going to the same places on holiday. Visit countries and environments that are unusual for you.

29
Ways to be more spontaneous at work

We are told that we should plan our lives, make to-do lists, work diligently, organize our schedules and arrange things in sound and sensible ways. But is it better to sometimes do the opposite and just be spontaneous?

Researchers Tonietto and Malkoc[19] at Ohio University in 2016 carried out 13 studies of leisure activities and found that scheduling an activity (vs. experiencing it impromptu) makes it feel less free-flowing and more work-like. They discovered that scheduling diminishes both the anticipation and enjoyment of the experience. The researchers found that maintaining the free-flowing nature of the activity by 'roughly scheduling' (without prespecified times) is much better.

Spontaneity does not just lead to more fun. It also leads to more creativity and innovation. In business a strict regime of hard work and meetings with no down-time leaves little or no bandwidth for fresh ideas and experimentation. Working from home has exacerbated this trend and has purged the casual conversations and serendipitous moments we can share in the office.

How can you embolden spontaneity and creativity at work? Here are some ideas:

A meeting with no agenda. Most regular meetings have the same agenda with little time for 'any other business' at the end. Occasionally try a meeting with no agenda. People turn up and chat about anything they want to. You can guide it a little by asking questions such as, 'Tell us something good or unexpected that has happened.'

Boost mixing. Encourage people to have a coffee or lunch with someone from another department – just to have a chat and learn what is happening elsewhere in the business.

The dose of reality. Each member of the senior team is given a different list of (say) six recent customers for your product or service. They have to phone and chat to at least four of them and ask questions about the client's experiences and suggestions for improvements. The group then shares their stories and learnings. This can lead to many important insights and ideas for innovations.

The random lunch. Once a month the chief has a lunch with people chosen at random from different departments. There is no agenda but in a more relaxed atmosphere the boss should learn some home truths about what is really happening at the grass roots.

Cross-departmental social events. It is often at the bar at the end of the day that the really good ideas surface so encourage mixing in a relaxed way at sports events, quizzes or social activities after work.

The random buddy. In larger organizations people are assigned a random buddy in a distant department. The buddy is not chosen by a manager but assigned at random using birthdays or social security numbers. Buddies meet to share experiences and exchange ideas.

People are inclined to retreat to their comfort zones and work hard at their tasks. This is fine up to a point, but it stifles creativity and the casual interactions that lead to good ideas. From time to time, it pays to break the routine and do something spontaneous. Encourage some fun. Plan the unplanned. Allocate some time to try something impromptu and do it on the spur of the moment.

30
Replace logic with emotion

We like to think that the world is a rational place and so we can approach it in a sensible, logical and rational way. In business we are trained to be analytical. We respect data, targets, percentages, market shares and ratios. MBA students analyse case studies with detailed spreadsheets. We frame problems in terms of metrics and numbers. For example, we might ask:

- How can we increase sales by 10 per cent?
- How can we double brand awareness in our target market?
- How can we reduce the time to develop new products from 10 months to 6 months?
- How can we improve productivity in the workplace?
- How can we reduce attrition rates for our key technical staff?

These are all good questions which start from an analytical and factual standpoint and will generate analytical thoughts and ideas. But we have to remember that our staff and our customers are people. And people are driven by feelings more than by numbers. So a fruitful avenue of approach is to replace logic with emotion and reframe each question. Instead, we might now ask:

- How can we make our customers much happier with our products and services?

- How can we get people to smile when they hear our brand name?

- How can we reduce the frustrations people feel in new product approvals and progress delays?

- How can we get rid of the things that annoy and irritate our people at work?

- How can we make our technical staff feel proud and happy to work here?

By starting from a more personal and emotional level we are likely to come up with more and different ideas. Anything we can do to make our customers or people feel delighted with us or proud of us is worth exploring. Any idea that stops our customers or people feeling angry, frustrated, disappointed or sad is also worth exploring.

At your next management meeting, for a change, focus on feelings and emotions rather than data and logic – try using the questions above. It will get you thinking in new ways. It will lead you to novel and productive ideas.

The same principles apply in other walks of life. If you want to get your child to eat vegetables or your granny to move into a smaller house or a friend to develop a healthier lifestyle, then you may have already discovered that logical arguments carry little weight. Think laterally about their feelings and emotions. Ask them how they feel. Tell stories about people in similar situations. Explore options that appeal to their sentiments and passions.

31
The open-minded quiz

How open-minded are you? Try this quiz.

Almost everyone considers that they are open-minded and receptive to new ideas. As a friend facetiously remarked, 'I know I'm open-minded and nobody will convince me otherwise.' We are sure that we are tolerant and impartial. It is others who are intolerant, blinkered and narrow-minded. It is very easy to fall into a rut where we cling to our own entrenched concepts of the world and subconsciously reject notions which might disturb our views.

Try this quick quiz to see how you rate as regards being open-minded. There are just ten questions to which you have to give Yes or No answers.

1 In the last twelve months have you changed your mind on any significant topic? Minor decisions on where to go or what to eat do not count. Have you changed your position on any big political, moral or societal issue?   **Yes/No**

2 Do you have one or more close friends of a different ethnicity from you?   **Yes/No**

3 Can you take on board criticism and change (yes) or do you push back?   **Yes/No**

4 Have you watched any foreign language films in the last year?   **Yes/No**

5 Have you made any new good friends in the last twelve months?   **Yes/No**

6 Do you try out a variety of newspapers and magazines (yes) or stick to the same two or three (no)? If you do not read newspapers that counts as a no.   **Yes/No**

7 In conversations do you generally prefer to listen (yes) or talk (no)?   **Yes/No**

8 Do you try new places each year on holiday (yes) or typically go to the same places as before (no)?   **Yes/No**

9 When it comes to decisions do you ponder and have doubts (yes) or are you decisive and certain of your choices (no)?   **Yes/No**

10 Do you try many different websites for news and information (yes) or visit the same short list of social media and news websites (no)?   **Yes/No**

Give yourself one point for every Yes answer. Then calculate your score. The higher the score the better.

0 to 3: Stuck in a rut – fresh thinking needed!

4 to 6: Somewhat and sometimes open-minded.

7 to 10: You are receptive to new thinking.

32
Ten things to do when you are stuck

We all get stuck from time to time – even lateral thinkers. You may have stopped writing the book you started. Maybe you are making no progress on a crucial venture. You keep putting something off. Your team cannot make headway on a project. Momentum has stalled and it is difficult to fire it up again. What can be done? Here is a ten-step plan to get things going.

Identify the barrier

Simply write down the main reason or reasons why you have stalled. Don't just say, 'I am too busy with other things.' Find the real reason why this is not a priority getting the action it needs. Why are you putting things off? Why have you lost enthusiasm? Is there some tangible or intangible obstacle? Once the barrier is clearly identified it is easier to see ways to overcome it.

Redefine the goal

Go back to basics. Ask, what are we trying to achieve here? What problem are we trying to solve and for whom? What benefits will it bring? We started this undertaking for a good reason. What was it and is it still valid? If it is no longer important then perhaps we should stop work on it altogether. But if it is still significant then we should clearly say so – to ourselves and to the group (if there is one). Let's remotivate ourselves by articulating the reasons for this project and the benefits it will bring.

Check your assumptions

What assumptions are we making here? About technology or customers or markets or needs or anything else. What if the assumptions are wrong? Is there a better, simpler, faster way to achieve our goal? Brainstorm this question.

Consider the opposite

As an extension of challenging assumptions why not consider doing the exact opposite? Instead of building a complicated expensive solution, maybe construct a simpler free one. Wikipedia, Uber and Airbnb all turned existing assumptions upside down.

Look for a metaphor

Who has faced a similar problem but in a different field? Can we find an analogy for our challenge and copy some of the methods that someone else used when they faced something similar?

Assume superpowers

We are stuck with a problem. Who could easily solve it and what would they do? How would Jeff Bezos or Elon Musk or Oprah Winfrey or Sir Richard Branson tackle this? Think of your favourite historical figure or fictional hero or movie superstar. Take on their attributes and come at the problem from a fresh direction.

Change the medium

Can we change something substantial in the current plan? If we are building a website, could we build an app instead? If we are writing a blog, could we offer a podcast in its place? Can we change the delivery mechanism, the medium, the technology or some other substantial component to overcome the roadblock?

Grab a resource

If you had an unlimited budget, what would you do with it? What is the single most important resource you need right now to get things moving? Identify the tool and then go and get it.

Call for help

Who could you ask for help? We often shy away from asking for assistance because we think it makes us look weak and needy. But asking for help is often the smartest thing to do. Is there someone more experienced, more technical, better connected or smarter than you who you can reach out to? Pick up the phone and ask them. Chances are they will be glad to help.

Consider starting over

You may have already invested time, money and effort into this project, but if you were to start again from scratch what would you do differently? Would you use different materials, different methods, different team members? Thinking about how you would start again with a blank sheet of paper can give you powerful pointers for things you should change.

Try these approaches and you should find that you can quickly getting moving again.

33

Improve your powers of persuasion

Would you like to be more persuasive with people? How can you get people to like you, respect you and listen to your suggestions? Here are some lateral hacks – easy techniques that can make a big difference. Studies have shown these four simple expressions to be highly effective when used in the right circumstances.

What I really like about you is _____

Tell someone something that you admire in them and they will like you for it. This works with your boss, your colleagues, your partner, your parents, your children – indeed just about everyone. Find something nice you can honestly say about them and say it. If your boss is a difficult, overbearing person to deal with, you can still find something good to say. 'What I really like about you is that you are always clear and decisive.' A variant on this is, 'What you are really good at is _____.' Everyone likes praise. You can always find something that is good about the other person. So start your conversation on a positive note by sincerely giving them credit. It will put them in a better and more receptive mood.

Please _____ *because* _____

Research in a large study at the University of Wisconsin found that the addition of a 'because' at the end of a request doubled the chance of getting a positive response. So you could say, 'Please give me your report by Tuesday.' But you are more likely to be successful if you say, 'Please give me your report by Tuesday because I really need it before the management meeting on Wednesday.' Similarly, you might say to your partner, 'Please come with me into town.' Then add, 'because I need some help choosing a new outfit.' Give people a reason to comply and it is more likely that they will.

But you are free to _____

Make your request. Push a little. Then reduce the pressure with a get-out phrase. 'I really think you should see the doctor about this, but you are free to carry on doing nothing if you want.' Research shows that taking the pressure off a little increases the chance that the other person will agree. Variants on the phrase include 'It is entirely up to you', 'You are not obliged', 'It is your choice.' So you might say, 'I firmly believe it is time to get a new and more reliable car but it is entirely up to you if you want to stick with the old one.'

If you _____, *then I* _____

This is a great phrase to use in any negotiation. Put the first obligation on the other party and then offer your exchange. 'If you do your homework then I will buy you an ice cream.' When the client asks for a better price you can say something like, 'If you can pay cash now then we can give a three per cent discount.' Don't start your negotiation by offering up a concession. Start with a request that you both move forward. Make your offer conditional on their action.

As we go through life we all have to try to secure agreement. We cannot just tell people what to do; we have to persuade them. Try using these tactics with conviction and sincerity. They will make you more convincing and persuasive.

34
Think like a criminal

Have you seen *The Day of the Jackal*? Edward Fox plays a professional assassin, the 'Jackal', who is hired to assassinate French President Charles de Gaulle. It is a compelling thriller in which it is hard not to admire the cunning and guile of the ruthless killer. In the end you feel disappointed that he did not succeed with his audacious plan.

It is an example of a genre of storytelling in which the main protagonist is a clever criminal. We seem to find them fascinating. *Breaking Bad* is about a chemistry teacher who becomes a master drugs dealer. *The Sopranos* is about a Mafia family. *Ozark* concerns a money launderer for a drugs gang. All these shows feature anti-heroes who are lawbreakers. They are people we should revile yet we are drawn to side with them. Why do we find them so enthralling? Perhaps it is because we secretly admire their daring, their risk-taking, their audacity and the crafty ways they avoid the law.

We disdain common criminals. We laugh at the dumb burglar who gets stuck in a window and drops his loot. But we have a grudging admiration for criminal masterminds. They are lateral thinkers and innovators. What lessons can we take from them to help us with our everyday problems?

- **They break the rules**. Criminals are prepared to break any rule and any law. We should obey the law but at the same time be prepared to challenge every rule and convention.

Travis Kalanick broke the rules of the taxi business when he founded a taxi company that had no taxis – Uber.

- **They exploit weaknesses.** Crooks look for flaws in security systems and then seek to exploit them. Sports coaches look for weaknesses in their opponents' set-ups. Generals look for weaknesses in the enemy positions. Marketing professionals look for weaknesses in their competitors' marketing. Business leaders and political leaders look for weaknesses in their rivals and at the same time must be aware of their own weaknesses which can be exploited.

- **They mislead and disguise.** A clever magician distracts you with one hand while picking your pocket with the other. Eisenhower put great efforts into misleading Hitler regarding his D-Day intentions. He feinted that he would invade at the Pas de Calais rather than in Normandy. Misdirection is a clever tactic in many a contest.

- **They take risks and accept failure.** An ambitious criminal takes calculated risks. He knows there is a danger that he will be caught and endure a spell in prison. It is an occupational hazard which he accepts. He tries and tries again. All great entrepreneurs and inventors are risk-takers. Many business founders have several flops before they hit on a winner. If we want more success then we should be prepared to take more risks, fail more often and learn from setbacks.

- **They think laterally.** Keep looking for a smarter alternative. Car thieves in Taiwan found an ingenious way to evade police while collecting ransoms from owners for the return of their vehicles. They used homing pigeons. They left a ransom note and a pigeon, promising to return the car if the bird was dispatched with cash in a can tied to its body. The police said, 'We tried to catch the thieves by using telescopes to follow the pigeon, but it flew too high and too fast, and we lost it.'[20]

I am not advocating that you become a criminal, but I am advocating that you sometimes think like a criminal. Protect yourself and your business by thinking how a criminal or a competitor could exploit your weaknesses. See fresh possibilities by challenging conventions and breaking the rules. It is fine to be an upright and steady citizen but sometimes it pays to be devious, lateral and cunning in your approach. Think like a criminal but stay inside the law!

And if you can think like a criminal it can help you to outwit them. Here are some lateral ideas to combat thieves.

Put up a 'Beware of the dog' sign, even if you do not have a pet. Burglars hate dogs.

Find clever hiding places. Most people put their jewellery in their bedside table, or in the wardrobe, or in a jewellery box. Find somewhere that is not obvious. You can buy little safes which look just like wall sockets.

Use decoys. On holiday take an old wallet with a few low value bills. Give it without complaint to any robber. Similarly at home put some costume jewellery and old watches inside a cheap jewellery box on your bedside table.

Take an old key that does not fit any of your locks and super-glue it to the step under your doormat. A thief will realize your trick and then look up to see your security camera. They will leave in a hurry.

35
Memory technique: Pegging a List

There are many tricks and techniques you can use to boost your memory and help you to recall important information. Sometimes you need to remember a list and be able to access it at any point. For instance, you might need to know what item 6 is, or item 11.

I recommend using this memory pegging technique. We 'peg' each item to a visual symbol for its number. The method I use is a rhyming approach. The list of pegs is as follows:

1 Ton (one ton)

2 Zoo

3 Tree

4 Door

5 Hive (with bees buzzing around)

6 Sticks

7 Heaven

8 Gate

9 Line (fishing line)

10 Den (e.g. the lion's den)

11 Soccer 11

12 Shelf

13 Hurting

14 Courting

15 Lifting

16 Licking

17 Leavening (baking bread)

18 Hating

19 Lightning

20 Plenty (horn of plenty)

Say our task was to remember the first 10 Presidents of the USA. They are:

1 George Washington

2 John Adams

3 Thomas Jefferson

4 James Madison

5 James Monroe

6 John Quincy Adams

7 Andrew Jackson

8 Martin Van Buren

9 William Harrison

10 John Tyler

Most people would find this a fairly difficult list to remember in sequence, but we can do so by associating the image of the number with an image for the surname. For example:

1 A one-ton weight balanced on top of the Washington Memorial.

2 Adam and Eve naked in a cage at the zoo.

3 An airplane crashed in a tree. (Jefferson Airplane was a pop group.)

4 We open a door and see Madison Avenue in New York in front of us.

5 Marilyn Monroe with her skirt billowing over a hive full of buzzing bees.

6 Adam is eating a fruit on a long stick. It is not an apple; it is a quince.

7 Michael Jackson performing his spacewalk dance in heaven.

8 A van has crashed into a gate. On the van is a bird – it is a blue wren.

9 We pull up our fishing line and find Harrison Ford on the end of it.

10 Daniel is in the lion's den. He is tiling the walls of the den.

The more dramatic or ridiculous the image the easier it is to remember. Now we can easily remember any of the first ten Presidents and know his number.

If you have to remember 40 or 60 items then you can do so by using a red list, a blue list and a yellow list, say. So 5 would be a red hive, 22 a blue zoo and 51 a yellow soccer team.

Try this method when you next have an important list to memorize. After a little practice you will be surprised at how well it works.

36

Memory technique: The virtual journey

Professional speakers use a simple and effective technique to flawlessly remember the topics they plan to cover in a speech. It is called the virtual journey. It enables you easily to remember a list in sequence. You take an imaginary journey around a familiar route – say your house, your road or your town – and you attach the things you want to remember to the places along the way.

Say for example you want to remember a sequence of key points for a conference speech you are giving. The first nine items are:

1 A description of how customers have problems with your products

2 A story about when you were at junior school

3 A quote from Abraham Lincoln

4 An anecdote about Barack Obama

5 An example of book marketing practice from Amazon

6 A statistic about 90 per cent of businesses

7 Your proposal for a new product or service

8 A list of some of the benefits – including happier customers

9 A call to action – what you want people to do

The route you decide to take is as follows:

1 Your bedroom

2 Your bathroom

3 On the stairs

4 In the downstairs toilet

5 In the kitchen

6 In the lounge

7 In the back garden

8 On your front drive

9 Outside your neighbour's house

So you might imagine a journey as follows. You find an angry customer in your bed – they are struggling with your product. You go into your bathroom and see a little boy at a desk – it is you. You go to the top of the stairs where you find Abraham Lincoln with his black hat and long beard walking up the stairs towards you. You descend to the downstairs toilet where you find Barack Obama sitting on the toilet. You go to the kitchen but find that it is filled from floor to ceiling with books – all from Amazon. You enter the lounge and see a huge number 90 written on the wall. You look out to the back garden where there is a large gleaming model of your new product. You walk to the front drive which you find thronged with happy customers. You push past them to your neighbour's house where you find a megaphone which you use to make your big appeal

When you come to make the speech, you simply make the mental journey on the route and all the items will spring into mind in the right sequence. Each one reminds you of the story you want to tell. Many professional speakers use this technique. You can use it to remember a speech, give a presentation or recall a list. You should make the visual images dramatic and memorable. With a little practice you will recall every detail flawlessly. People will be really impressed that you could remember every important point without any notes.

37
Better a giraffe than a zebra

Zebra stands for Zero Evidence But Really Adamant. 'Zebras' are people who see things in black and white. They are sure of their own opinions, and they disdain information, facts or science that undermine their beliefs. Donald Trump was a zebra and he famously dismissed countervailing reports as 'fake news'.

Tom Nichols writes in his book *The Death of Expertise* that ignorance is now seen as a virtue: 'To reject the advice of experts is to assert autonomy, a way for people to demonstrate independence from nefarious elites and to insulate their fragile egos from ever being told that they are wrong.'[21]

A poll by the *Washington Post* in 2014 asked Americans if they favoured US military intervention in Ukraine.[22] Only one in six of those polled could place Ukraine on a map but nonetheless they were sure that action was needed. Similarly, a Public Policy Poll in 2015 asked American voters if they supported bombing Agrabah.[23] Nearly one third of Republican voters said they did, but Agrabah does not exist – except in the Disney film *Aladdin*. A study by Ohio State University in 2015 found that both liberals and conservatives tended to discount science which contradicted their views.[24] When faced with the data they would typically question the validity of the research rather than reconsider their own beliefs.

We saw many zebras with strongly entrenched opinions in the Brexit debate. Zebras defy the science of climate change or of vaccination. Others are adamant supporters of homeopathy although there is no scientific evidence for it. Similarly in business we encounter CEOs who are brimming with hubris and self-confidence in their long-held opinions despite all the customer research that shows things have changed.

Of course, experts can be wrong, and we should challenge them and test the validity of their assumptions and methods. But it is dangerous to ignore them and trust solely to our instincts. The captain of the Titanic ignored warnings about icebergs and raced on to disaster.

So don't be a zebra. Much better to be a giraffe. Giraffes are far-sighted, humble and open-minded. They survey the landscape, take in the facts and see dangers as well as opportunities. After due consideration they stick their necks out and make decisions. They head off in that direction but are quite capable of turning around and admitting that they were wrong. The lateral thinker is a giraffe, open-minded and receptive to challenging ideas. They are capable of questioning their most cherished beliefs.

We need more giraffes and fewer zebras – especially at senior levels.

38
Messy beats tidy

It is claimed that Albert Einstein said, 'If a cluttered desk is a sign of a cluttered mind, of what, then, is an empty desk a sign?'

We are encouraged at home, at school and at work to be tidy and ordered. Many companies have a clean desk policy. But there is much evidence that messy people are more creative and that messy environments can spur the imagination. Mark Twain, Virginia Woolf, Mark Zuckerberg, Steve Jobs, Tony Hsieh and Einstein himself were all renowned for their cluttered desks.

Eric Abrahamson and David H Freedman say: 'Mess isn't necessarily the absence of order. A messy desk can be a highly effective prioritizing and accessing system. On a messy desk, the more important, urgent work tends to stay close by and near the top of the clutter, while the safely ignorable stuff tends to get buried to the bottom or near the back, which makes perfect sense.'[25]

In 2013 researchers Kathleen Vohs, Joseph Redden and Ryan Rahinel published a paper entitled 'Physical Order Produces Healthy Choices, Generosity, and Conventionality, Whereas Disorder Produces Creativity'.[26] In one experiment they found that participants in a disorderly room were more creative than participants in an orderly room.

In his book *Messy*, economist Tim Harford argues that we are wrong to strive for order and tidiness because openness, adaptability and creativity are inherently messy.[27] We should appreciate the benefits of untidiness. He gives the example of the distinguished jazz pianist Keith Jarrett, who was asked to play a concert on a piano that he found to be sub-standard. It was too quiet and the notes in the high registers did not play well. At first he refused, but then he relented and produced an outstanding and original piece of work. Being restricted to sub-standard equipment forced him to improvise in clever ways.

The German General Erwin Rommel relished chaotic situations because he believed he could think and react faster than his enemy. While his opponents were carefully preparing their next plan, Rommel would launch an unexpected attack – often from an unpromising position. He believed that the more uncertainty and chaos he could cause the better. Harford goes on to compare Jeff Bezos's early actions with Amazon and Donald Trump's surprise tactics in the Republican primaries with Rommel's unconventional and messy approach.

Researchers Katherine Phillips, Katie Liljenquist and Margaret Neale ran an experiment where they compared the problem-solving abilities of teams.[28] Some groups comprised four friends; others comprised three friends and one stranger. The groups containing the strangers did much better. Interestingly, when the groups self-assessed, the groups of friends wrongly thought that they had done well and the groups with the stranger wrongly thought that they had done less well. We become complacent in homogeneous groups – outsiders help to challenge our thinking. Team harmony is overrated.

The great strengths of big cities are their assorted communities and the messy connections that these can throw up. Diverse cities and diverse economies do better and are more resilient than those that specialize in one or two sectors only.

Teachers tell us that children learn more from informal games where they have to improvise and make up their own rules than from standard games where the rules are clear.

Harford's thesis is summed up in this quote from his book: 'We have seen again and again that real creativity, excitement and humanity lie in the messy parts of life, not the tidy ones.'

If we want to be lateral thinkers then we should welcome messy desks, diverse communities and random happenings.

39
Mix with more creative people

According to the late US entrepreneur Jim Rohn, you are the average of the five people you spend the most time with. The people you associate with help shape what you think and who you are. We tend to congregate with friends who are like us in background, interests, education, attitudes and opinions. This is comfortable and reassuring but it inhibits creativity or independent thought. Instead it encourages conformity and groupthink. You and your friends probably agree about most things. Normal people have normal ideas. If you want to be lateral, different and creative then you need to widen your circle to include a great diversity of people. And they should not all be people you like. You should immerse yourself into a world of awkward conversations, disparate ideas, intellectual challenge and contrarian thinkers.

Hans Christian Andersen's fairy tales have captivated generations with their strange themes and inspirational characters. His classic stories include 'The Ugly Duckling', 'The Princess and the Pea' and 'The Emperor's New Clothes'. The Disney film *Frozen* is based on Andersen's story 'The Snow Queen'. Andersen had an unhappy childhood. His grandfather was committed to a lunatic asylum. The boy would often visit him there and spent time listening to the wild ramblings of the patients – this was a source for many of his stories. He escaped conventional company by visiting a psychiatric hospital.

Andy Warhol kept open house. Anyone could hang out in his studio. Many creative people congregated there. They often made suggestions for new works of art or helped to create them. Warhol soaked up their ideas. The place became a hotbed of inventiveness and imagination. Among his visitors were the musician Lou Reed and the Velvet Underground.

This approach has been copied by other artists but also by creative agencies who want the buzz of different ingenious people batting ideas around. Can you go and meet people in a place that is the equivalent of Andersen's lunatic asylum or Warhol's studio?

Some creative geniuses work alone but many work in tandem. John Lennon and Paul McCartney often clashed but they contributed great ideas to each other's songs. When TV producers want a new soap opera or a comedy show they commission a group of different scriptwriters who work, argue and laugh together. They spark off each other.

If you want creative ideas then mix with creative people. Search through your network and see if you know anyone who is a composer, an artist, a writer, an architect, an actor, a producer or an entertainer. Who do you know who is a radical thinker? Which person can give you original opinions and stimulating ideas? Go out of your way to cultivate these acquaintances. Discuss things with them. When you are working on some creative project openly ask for their input. I guarantee they will give you something more valuable than you get from your five best friends.

40

Questions to ask yourself after a setback

We all fail. As we go through life, we have relationships that don't work out, jobs that just aren't right, exams that we flunk, initiatives that don't succeed. The more new things we try the more failures we are likely to have. In fact, the only way to avoid failure is to do nothing new. So lateral thinkers will have many setbacks.

The important thing is how we deal with failure. It can be part of a downward slide in which lack of confidence reinforces feelings of inadequacy and incompetence. But experiencing failure can be a learning experience and an opportunity for a fresh start. A good way to begin this process is by asking yourself some tough questions.

1 **What can I learn from this?** Take responsibility for what went wrong. OK, so it was not all your fault – but some of it was. Successful people don't make excuses or blame others. They take ownership of the issues. Be critical but constructive. Try to look at the experience objectively. Make a list of the key things that happened. Analyse the list step by step and look for the learning points.

2 **What could I have done differently?** What other options did you have? What choices did you make? How could you have handled it differently? With the benefit of hindsight, what different steps would you have taken?

3 Do I need to acquire or improve some skills? Did the problem reveal some lack of skill on your part? How could you learn or improve those skills? Perhaps there are books or courses or people you could turn to. Make a self-development plan to acquire the skills and experiences you need.

4 Who can I learn from? Is there someone to whom you can turn to for advice? Did a boss, colleague or a friend see what happened? If they are constructive and supportive then ask them for some feedback and guidance. Most people do not ask for help because they believe it to be a sign of weakness rather than strength. It's not. It shows that you are ready to learn and change. Any good friend will be happy to help.

5 What will I do next? Now draw up an action plan. Will you try something similar or something different? Revisit your goals and objectives. This reversal has been a setback on your journey but think of it as a diversion rather than a halt. You can now reset your sights on your destination and plan a new course.

If you read the life stories of successful people – especially inventors, explorers, scientists or statesmen – you will find that their early careers are littered with failures. Walt Disney, Thomas Edison and Henry Ford are typical examples. Abraham Lincoln suffered many defeats in his career in politics including losing the nomination for Vice President in 1856 and his second run at being a US Senator in 1858. Two years later he was elected President.

The important point is to use your setbacks as learning experiences and make them stepping stones to future success. There are always positives you can take from every episode in your life. Asking yourself these five questions can help find them.

41
Lateral thinking in mathematics

One of the world's greatest mathematicians, Carl Friedrich Gauss, was born in Germany in 1777. It is said that when he was a young boy at school the teacher wanted to keep the class quiet, so he set this problem: 'Add up all the numbers from one to one hundred.' The schoolmaster thought that this task of adding 100 numbers would secure a long silence but, in a flash, the young Gauss raised his hand with the answer. He had found a quick and elegant way to solve the problem and what he did is an example of lateral thinking in mathematics. The obvious way to tackle the problem is to add 1 + 2 + 3 + 4 and so on. Gauss saw that if he added 1 + 100 he got 101, if he added 2 + 99 he got 101, if he added 3 + 98 he got 101, and so on all the way to 50 + 51. There are 50 sets of 101 so the answer is 5050.

Try this problem. Train A sets off from Reading straight towards London at 10 miles per hour. At the same time Train B sets off from London straight towards Reading at 20 miles per hour. London and Reading are 30 miles apart. Immediately that Train A sets off, a fly on the front of the train flies straight towards Train B at 50 miles per hour. Once it reaches the oncoming train it immediately turns and flies back to Train A. It then flies back to Train B and so on covering ever-decreasing distances until the two trains pass. How far does the fly fly in total?

One way to solve this problem is to calculate and sum each of the journeys made by the fly. This is complex, difficult and tedious. But there is a much simpler and easier way to solve the problem. The two trains approach each other at a combined speed of 30 mph over a distance of 30 miles. So it takes them one hour to meet. The fly flies at a constant 50 mph. Therefore in one hour it flies 50 miles. Simple!

Mathematics is one of the purest, most abstract, most challenging and most useful of human intellectual endeavours. It can be highly theoretical, but it is also a crucial tool to solve practical real-world problems in science, engineering, architecture and many other fields. Mathematics offers great opportunities for lateral thinking and mathematicians love to find elegant, fresh ways to solve tricky problems.

A good example of the use of lateral thinking in mathematics is imaginary numbers (also known as complex numbers). These are numbers that by definition cannot exist – yet they are really useful! What is the square root of 9? You will probably say 3. And you would be right, but a mathematician would say it is plus or minus 3. Because if you square either +3 or –3 you get +9. So what is the square root of –9? We have long assumed that all numbers are either positive or negative (except maybe zero). But if you multiply a positive number by itself, you get a positive number, and similarly if you multiply a negative number by itself you get a positive number. So no real number multiplied by itself can make –9. This was the received wisdom in mathematics from ancient times until the Renaissance, when Italian mathematician Gerolamo Cardano published a book called *Ars Magna* in 1545. In it he showed a clever trick for solving cubic equations. It involved using a symbol for the square root of –1. This became known as i – standing for imaginary. It soon became apparent that by using this illusory number it was possible to unravel all sorts of problems in many different fields. Indeed, today imaginary numbers are used to solve equations everywhere from economics to quantum physics.

Now it is your turn. Try to do some lateral thinking with these three questions. (They are taken from the easier sections of *Mathematical Lateral Thinking Puzzles* by Paul Sloane and Des MacHale.[29])

1 You have two glasses of the same size, one half full of wine and the other half full of water. You take a spoonful of wine and mix it into the water. Then you take a spoonful of the mixture and mix it into the water. Is there more wine in the water now than there is water in the wine?

2 In a knockout singles tennis tournament there are 79 entries. How many matches must be played to decide the winner?

3 A poor little snail is at the bottom of a well 30 feet deep. Every day it climbs up three feet but every night it falls back two feet again. How many days does it take the snail to reach the top of the well?

Answers on page 229.

42
Beware these cognitive biases

A cognitive bias is a persistent error in the system of thinking. We all suffer to some extent from cognitive biases which affect our judgements. Fortunately, psychologists have studied these phenomena and have given us the opportunity to be aware of these thinking flaws and so to counteract them. Here are some common cognitive biases which the lateral thinker will detect in themselves and in others.

Affinity bias. We tend to be favourably disposed toward people most like ourselves. We value their opinions and judgements above others.

Anchoring bias. We incline to rely too heavily on the very first piece of information we receive. For example, if you show someone a car and ask if they think it is worth more than £1,000, and then ask them to estimate its value, they will typically give a much lower value than if you first ask them if they think it is worth less than £10,000. You can use this bias to set the expectations of others by putting the first bid on the table in any negotiation.

Authority bias. The propensity to defer to authority and not to use reason to challenge decisions.

Availability bias. This involves placing greater value on information which is recent or which comes to mind quickly. We give greater credence to information that is immediately available and tend to overestimate the probability of similar things happening in the future.

Confirmation bias. The tendency to search for and value information that confirms our beliefs and preconceptions and to reject or ignore information that challenges or negates our beliefs and opinions.

Conservatism. The belief that it is always better to avoid risk.

Gambler's fallacy. The belief that bad luck will be followed by good luck. For example, after a coin lands heads five times in a row you might believe that tails is more likely on the next throw. But if the coin is fair, there is still a 50/50 chance of heads.

Halo effect. Our overall impression of a person influences how we feel and think about their character, opinions and decisions. In particular, their physical attractiveness can influence how we rate their other qualities. The views of the tall confident handsome man are given more weight than they deserve.

Law of large numbers. We can be led astray by results from small samples. Sample size is critical to confidence in statistical results.

Overconfidence. We tend to overrate our own capability to make correct decisions.

Risk compensation. When people feel safer they can be more at risk. Cyclists who wear helmets have more accidents than those who do not.

Social proof. If lots of other people are doing it, then it must be the right choice. But the crowd can be very wrong.

Triviality law. We prefer to discuss trivial issues which are simple to understand and easy to fix rather than important issues which are complex and difficult to solve.

There are some things that you can do to help overcome cognitive biases that might impair your judgement and decision making. First, be aware of how these tendencies might affect your thinking. Read the list and objectively assess which ones you might suffer from. Secondly, consider your decision-making style and process. For instance, are you overly self-confident or risk-averse? Thirdly, deliberately challenge your biases – take an opposite standpoint and force yourself to think differently.

Part Five
Lateral thinking at work

43

Get someone else to do the work

One of the most famous scenes in Mark Twain's *Adventures of Tom Sawyer* occurs when Tom has to whitewash a fence as a punishment. His friend Ben Rogers comes along to ridicule him about having to work. Tom ignores him and concentrates on painting, so Ben eventually asks if he likes doing it. Tom replies, 'Like it? Well, I don't see why I oughtn't to like it. Does a boy get a chance to whitewash a fence every day?' When Ben asks if he could have a go, Tom reluctantly agrees and eventually he has a gang of boys pay him small amounts for the privilege of painting the fence. It is an example of lateral thinking in action. Tom turned the situation around by persuading Ben and the other boys to feel pleased to get the chance to paint the fence.

In years gone by you had to queue at the airport check-in desk so that the clerk could register your details and print your boarding card. Then someone had a bright idea. Get the passenger to enter all their details at home on their computer or via an app, choose their seat and print a boarding pass or download it to their phone. This saved time for passengers without luggage. It also saved the airline the task of checking them in. The airline had transferred part of the job to the customer. It was a win-win and became universally adopted as a better practice.

Sales of cake mix were flat in the US in the 1950s. A researcher, Ernest Dichter, carried out a study for General Mills. After interviewing women, Dichter reported that the very simplicity of mixes – just add water and stir – led to women feeling guilty that they had done virtually nothing. He advised that the cook should have something to do – adding eggs to the mix. According to Dichter, General Mills and other cake mix makers followed this advice and left out dried eggs. Women added their own fresh eggs, felt better about the process and sales increased.[30] It should be added that his view of the reasons for the success of the idea has been challenged by some commentators who point out that cakes made with fresh eggs just tasted better!

Part of Ikea's success lies in the way in which it transferred the job of assembling furniture to the customer. This allowed the items to be flat-packed and reduces storage and transportation costs. People could save money by doing part of the work themselves.

It is reported that wild crows have been enlisted to pick up discarded cigarette butts from the streets of Stockholm.[31] The birds are rewarded with food every time they drop a cigarette butt into a receptacle which includes an automatic peanut dispenser. It is believed that using the birds could save 75 per cent of the current costs of clearing up cigarette butts in the city. The crows are quick leaners and do not eat the rubbish. Experts estimate that crows have the reasoning skills of a seven-year-old child.

Giffgaff is a UK-based mobile phone network which benefits from community support. Technical questions are answered by other users, members of the support community, who gain small rewards for their work.

Outer is a garden furniture supplier. They do not have showrooms or retail premises. If you want to see what the goods look like you can find from their website a customer nearby who is happy to show you their furniture. The customer is rewarded for any sale made. The company saves on expensive showrooms by getting clients to provide the displays.

Maybe you cannot get a crow, or another animal, or a customer or a gang of boys to do part of your work, but there is probably someone you can ask. Analyse all the low-value tasks that you spend time on and ask whether it would be smarter to get someone else to do the job. Should you be spending time on bookkeeping, website maintenance, arranging appointments or phoning suppliers? Would it be better to pay a specialist to do these jobs while you focus on what you are really good at and get paid for?

44

Repurpose your product

Have you ever used a knife as a screwdriver or a shoe as a hammer? If so you repurposed a product for an application that the producer did not foresee. You put the product to another use. This idea can be a fruitful source of innovations for your product or service if you only you can think laterally.

De Beers is a diamond mining company founded in South Africa in 1888. It specialized in industrial diamonds which were used as drill bits – because diamonds are the hardest things found in nature. In a brilliant piece of marketing, it repurposed diamonds as symbols of love and devotion. De Beers created the concept of the diamond engagement ring – with the slogan 'A diamond is forever.' It has been voted the best advertising slogan of the 20th century.

Kleenex tissues were developed to remove make-up and cold cream. The Kleenex company discovered that people were buying the tissues to blow their noses. The entire marketing strategy was changed with the marketing slogan 'Don't carry a cold in your pocket.'

Dasparkhotel, in the town of Ottensheim, Austria, sits on the banks of the river Danube. This unique hotel in a park is a collection of five freestanding cylindrical rooms made from repurposed urban sewage drainage pipes. Each seven-foot-wide room contains a double bed, lamp, storage space, bedding and a power outlet. Just like in a campsite, toilets and showers are located nearby and guests can swim in the adjacent 'swimming pool' – the Danube.

Lucozade is an orange-flavoured carbonated drink invented by an English pharmacist in 1927. It was promoted as a health drink and sold in pharmacies. Its advertising tag line was 'Lucozade aids recovery'. Mothers bought it for their sick children. Over time the brand was successfully repositioned as a sports and energy drink. The same product was promoted with different benefits to a different market.

Mobile phones are no longer primarily phones. They are used as cameras, browsers and app players – on which you can occasionally make or receive a call. They have been put to other uses.

Swarfega is a thick gelatinous heavy-duty hand cleaner that removes grease and dirt. It was invented in 1947 by Audley Williamson, an industrial chemist who had founded a detergent company in Belper, Derbyshire. His new product was designed to extend the life of silk stockings. However, the success of nylon stockings in replacing silk ones knocked a big hole in his market. He heard that mechanics had found the new product useful for cleaning their hands. The product was repurposed and became the prime choice as a hand cleaner in engineering companies.

In SCAMPER, a powerful brainstorming technique in which seven verbs are used to generate fresh ideas for a product, the P stands for 'Put to other use'. The team has to generate many ideas for entirely different applications. I find that a good way to start the session is to ask, 'If a law were passed which made the current use of our product illegal, what completely different use could we find for it?' If diamonds were banned from use as drill bits, could we conceive of using them in engagement rings?

Observe your customers. How are they using your product? Are there any unusual or offbeat applications? If some people are using your knife as a screwdriver or your shoe as a hammer, then maybe that is a source of an innovative new application and new market.

45
The founding of Google

Lateral thinking involves trying new approaches, borrowing ideas from other places, asking 'What if' questions and recognizing when you have stumbled on something interesting.

In 1973 Carl and Gloria Page, who both worked at Michigan State University, had a son. Carl was a Professor of Computer Science and Gloria taught programming. They called their son Lawrence, but he was known as Larry. At the age of six the boy was given a home computer, one of the very first models, and soon he was programming. Larry was a precocious child and went on to study business and computer science at his parent's university. He then applied to MIT but was rejected so instead he went to Stanford, which proved a happy choice. It was during his orientation programme in 1995 that he met second-year graduate student Sergey Brin. The two hit it off and became friends. They were both smart, rebellious and geeky. They argued a lot. Page later said, 'I thought Sergey was pretty obnoxious. He had really strong opinions about things, and I guess I did, too.'[32]

Brin was born in Moscow in 1974. Both his parents were mathematicians but their prospects in Russia were limited because they were Jewish. In 1979 they emigrated to the US. In a similar fashion to Larry Page, the young Sergey received a Commodore 64 as a present and programmed it. He graduated from the University of Maryland with a degree in mathematics and computer science. In another significant coincidence he also was rejected by MIT before going to Stanford.

They were both fascinated by the World Wide Web which was exploding in use in the mid-1990s. Page's dissertation topic was how to assess the relative importance of different webpages. He borrowed an idea from his parent's world – academic research. One way to judge the importance of a research paper is to count how many other research papers reference it as a source. Page wanted to do something with webpages but although it was easy to see how many links went *out* from a page it was not easy to see how many other sites linked *to* it. Then he conceived an audacious question: 'What if we could download the whole of the World Wide Web and analyse all its links?'

At that time in early 1996 there were over 100,000 web sites, with over 10 million documents and around a billion links. And it was growing exponentially. Page was undaunted. He built a web crawler, a program which went through site by site and stored links and addresses. The project was called Backrub and it quickly grew to huge proportions. It absorbed over half of Stanford's entire web bandwidth and caused the university server to crash, but the university authorities were lenient and allowed him to continue. Brin was amazed at the boldness of the project and eagerly joined in.

They were still building a web analysis tool. Page later said, 'Amazingly, I had no thought of building a search engine. The idea wasn't even on the radar.' They built smarter ways to assess the value of a page based on the number and quality of incoming links. It then dawned on them that they had discovered the basis for a search engine of higher value than anything else around. They developed their approach so that they not only counted the number of incoming links but assigned a higher value to a link coming from a site with many incoming links. This was a novel and recursive method which gave greater accuracy in assessing the relative importance of sites.

Page and Brin called their search engine Google. They wanted to use the word *googol* which is the number 1 followed by 100 zeros. But Googol.com was already taken so they settled for Google.com. In April 1998 they published a paper explaining their approach without giving away the exact details.

In order to commercialize the project, they approached the CEOs of the leading search companies of the day – Yahoo, Alta Vista, Lycos and Excite. They presented their case and asked for $1 million to license their patents and tools. In each case they were turned down. Page said later, 'It was not a significant expense to them. But it was a lack of insight at the leadership level. A lot of them told us, "Search is not that important."' Why did the big players make such a mistake? They believed that the key to gaining traffic and advertising was to add more content. They thought that people would explore the web rather than search the web.

Page and Brin founded Google in 1998. It went on to wipe out all the big players who had turned down the two students.

Sometimes you stumble on to a great innovation. The geeky students did not set out to create a search engine but were smart enough to see the potential when it emerged.

46

Tony Hsieh – the remarkable cultural innovator at Zappos

Tony Hsieh (pronounced Shay) was born in 1973 in Illinois. His parents were immigrants from Taiwan who met at graduate school. Hsieh studied computer science at Harvard University where he was a member of a prize-winning programming contest team. While there, as a student job he managed a pizza grill. One of his customers was Alfred Lin, who became his friend and later became CFO and COO at Zappos. After graduating, Hsieh worked for Oracle but quit in 1996 after just five months to co-found the LinkExchange, an advertising network. It sold banner ads and grew quickly on the crest of the burgeoning wave of new websites. In 1998 LinkExchange was sold to Microsoft for $265 million.

Hsieh and his friend Alfred Lin then co-founded Venture Frogs, an incubator and investment firm. A friend had dared Hsieh to start a company with the name Venture Frogs so that is what he did. They invested in a variety of tech and internet start-ups, including the question-answering platform Ask Jeeves, the restaurant booking service OpenTable and Zappos, an online shoe retailer. A little later, in 2000, Hsieh joined Zappos as the CEO.

He was concerned that customers would feel nervous about buying shoes unseen and untried, so he set out to make them feel comfortable and secure with shopping online. Zappos offered free shipping and free returns. Initially he wanted to test the concept of selling shoes online. He had little capital but advertised a broad range of shoes, many of which were not in stock. When a customer ordered a pair of shoes Hsieh or his people would dash out and buy the item at a high street shop and then dispatch them. He made a loss on every such sale but quickly learnt what appealed to the type of people who buy online.

The company gained a reputation for extraordinary customer service. Hsieh empowered and encouraged employees to go to great lengths to help clients. This proved successful. When Hsieh joined Zappos in 2000 it had a turnover of $1.6 million. By 2009, he had grown revenues to $1 billion. At that point, Amazon acquired Zappos.com for $1.2 billion. Hsieh made at least $200 million from the sale but stayed on as CEO to lead the company.

He upended the company structure. In 2013 it became a company without job titles, where employees could self-organize. Zappos was listed in *Fortune* as one of the best companies to work for. Tony believed that having fun at work wasn't a liability; it was an asset.

The remarkable culture which Hsieh developed at Zappos starts with the hiring process which is longer and more involved than traditional recruitment. The company hires only about one per cent of all applicants. Before an employee is hired, they will meet several different employees and attend a company event. Zappos hires slowly with the emphasis on cultural fit.

New hires spend their first few weeks answering phones in the call centre learning how to respond to customer needs. This is useful training because in busy times all employees are expected to be available to answer the phones. Part of the induction process is a scavenger hunt to meet people and to find things out about the company.

Upon completion of their training, new employees encounter a rather lateral intervention: they are offered $3,000 to leave the company. This is a test of commitment. Zappos does not want people who do not love the job. If they turn down the exit offer, new employees have a 'graduation ceremony' with all the department present and cheering.

Zappos has a culture book that is written and updated by employees. It expresses how staff feel about the Zappos culture and the actions they take to develop it. This book is given to visitors and anyone else who wants it.

The company has a wide range of social activities for employees and their families including cook-outs, picnics and theatre trips. Managers make cultural assessments rather than performance evaluations and give raises based on skill tests.

Call centre staff are empowered to use their imagination to serve customers and make them happy. Evidence of the effectiveness of this approach is shown by the fact that over 75 per cent of sales are from repeat customers. One of the company's core values is to 'be adventurous, creative and open-minded'. The Zappos unique ethos has been carefully developed to enable employees to achieve that goal. The company is famous for encouraging people to express their creativity and for allowing them to fail.

Zappos shares its approach freely. In 2010 Tony Hsieh wrote a book, *Delivering Happiness*, which described the history and culture at Zappos.[33] It reached No 1 on the *New York Times* Best Seller List and stayed on the list for

27 weeks. Zappos has been so celebrated for its corporate values that the company has a consulting team which helps other businesses improve their cultures. It offers leadership training courses including the 'School of Wow'.

Hsieh loved the game of poker and it informed his business philosophy. He moved Zappos to downtown Las Vegas to be closer to the poker tables. In an article in *HuffPost* he expressed some business precepts he had learnt from poker:

- Act weak when strong, act strong when weak. Know when to bluff.
- Table selection is the most important decision you can make.
- Always be prepared for the worst possible scenario.
- The guy who never loses a hand is not the guy who makes the most money in the long run.[34]

He organized a major redevelopment and revitalization project for the dilapidated downtown area of Las Vegas. In 2013 he pledged $350 million for the project. Initially this was a plan for a place where Zappos employees could live and work, but the vision grew to create an environment where hundreds of small business and entrepreneurs could flourish.

In August 2020, Hsieh retired as CEO of Zappos after 21 years in charge. Tragically, in November 2020 he was injured in a house fire in New London, Connecticut. He was rescued by firefighters and taken to hospital but died later, two weeks before his 47th birthday.

Hsieh did many clever things to surprise and delight his customers. He instilled into the company a culture of outstanding service and fun. He empowered his staff to try new things. He was a lateral thinker and an outstanding entrepreneur.

47
Turn a weakness into a strength

We all have strengths and weaknesses; people do, countries do, companies do, and products do. People with closed minds can be oblivious to their failings but open-minded thinkers can coolly assess their weaknesses. The obvious things to do are to minimize your weakness or to add things which compensate for it. A more lateral approach is to emphasize your limitation and turn it into a strength. How can you do this? Let's look at an example.

A pint of Guinness takes much longer to pour than other beers and this might be seen as a weakness, but the Guinness marketing team chose to focus their advertising on this slow pouring and the anticipation of the drinker. They used the slogan 'Great things come to those who wait.' Similarly, Heinz ketchup is more viscous and slower to pour than other ketchups, so Heinz advertising and promotions focused on this as a sign of the excellence of the product. They implied that a runny ketchup was lower quality.

Jürgen Klinsmann was a wonderful German footballer who came to England to play for Tottenham Hotspur in 1994. Initially he was unpopular with fans because he had a reputation for 'diving' – faking a foul in order to win a free-kick or penalty. He cleverly turned this around. After he scored a great goal he did a comical dive on to the pitch in a parody of himself. From then whenever he or his team-mates scored a goal, they did the dive and fans loved it – and him.

Many companies have problems with long wait times for people dialling in to speak to them. The clothing company Zappos, mentioned in the previous chapter, turned around the problem by having different humorous messages on their customer service helplines. Every day a different employee hosts the phone calls and gets a chance to show their creativity. An example on Hallowe'en featured this recorded message:

> Trick or treat, smell my feet, Zappos customer service can't be beat. Hi, my name is Amber, and my name is Kimberly, from our product information support team, and we'll be hosting today's daily greeting on this spooky October 31st.

Every call ends with 'Press 4 to hear Zappos' Joke of the Day.' Two more employees tell you a joke. Zappos has turned the traditional problem of the helpline queue into a word-of-mouth marketing success.

The Leaning Tower of Pisa is famous because of its flaw. What flaws does your product have? List them and then brainstorm ways to turn them into features that you can exploit. Is there a clever way for you to turn a weakness into a strength?

48
Move the kettle!

Alex Pentland, a professor at MIT, combined staff identity badges with GPS positioning technology. This enabled him to observe the movements of workers in an office much in the same way as we might watch streams of ants crossing the ground. His findings are included in his book *Social Physics*.[35] He notes: 'Email has very little to do with productivity or creative output. I have found that the number of opportunities for social learning, usually through informal face-to-face interactions, is the largest single factor in corporate productivity.' He goes on to say, 'Most of the time, in most places, innovation is a group phenomenon. The most creative people are actually people who go around and collect ideas from lots of different people, play with them and bounce them off other people.'

You might have a great idea in the shower or driving to work. But to develop and improve that idea you need direct conversations with your fellows. It becomes a bit like a jazz jam session where one musician starts a theme and the other band members pick it up and take it in different directions. It follows that you should encourage social mixing, chat and collaboration in the workplace.

Bruce Daisley was European Vice President for Twitter and became host of the popular business podcast *Eat, Sleep, Work, Repeat*. In 2020 he published *The Joy of Work*.[36] In the book he gives 30 pieces of advice to 'fix your work culture and help you fall in love with your job again'. One of the tips is based on Pentland's work (as discussed above). It is this: move the kettle. If you want to improve collaboration and innovation, then think hard about the location of the water cooler, the coffee machine and the kettle. If you want two departments to work better together, then put a shared resource like the kettle between them. Set up soft spaces, maybe with sofas, to encourage informal discussions. And if you encourage people to work from home and to rely on email communication, then you are inhibiting innovation and collaboration.

The style, layout and decoration of your office rooms can influence people in unexpected ways. The researcher Ruth Haag argues that round tables lead to long discussion whereas rectangular tables lead to faster decisions.

Perhaps unsurprisingly, meetings without chairs have been found to take about one-third less time than normal meetings.

Researchers have discovered that the height of the ceiling in a meeting room can affect the outcome of the meeting.[37] Apparently a high ceiling encourages people to think more creatively while a low ceiling discourages imagination and influences people to think in a constrained way. So if you want an effective brainstorm choose somewhere with plenty of headroom. And wall colours matter. Neutral colours like grey or white subdue energy and enthusiasm. Nancy Kwallek, director of the University of Texas' interior design pro-gramme, found that these colours can lead to more errors. A better choice for the walls is a light shade of blue-green. This promotes feelings of calm, peace, sky and sea.[38]

49

Focus on the opportunity, not the problem

Two groups of engineering students were given a similar task – to design a bicycle rack for a car. The first group was shown an existing but poorly designed roof rack for bicycles. They looked at all the issues with the current design and then set out to come up with something better. The second group was not shown the ineffective roof rack; they were simply told to design a really good bicycle rack. The second group came up with much more elegant and effective designs. The first group focused on the problems with the existing design and that constrained their thinking.

The study was carried out by researchers David Jansson and Steven Smith and is mentioned in David Niven's book *It's Not About the Shark*.[39] That title refers to the problem which the then unknown director Steven Spielberg had in 1974 while shooting *Jaws*. The movie script involved many scenes showing a monster shark but the mechanical model shark they used had recurring technical faults and kept failing. The movie was running well behind schedule and over budget. The problem was that the shark just would not work. Spielberg did some lateral thinking. He removed the shark from all the initial scenes and implied its presence with the brilliant musical theme written by John Williams. Moviegoers found that what they imagined beneath the water was remarkably frightening. Critics and audiences raved about the film which kick-started Spielberg's rise to stardom.

When we are confronted with a problem, we tend to focus all our efforts on the features of the problem itself, rather than looking at the entire situation and the opportunities it offers. Focusing on the problem limits our possibilities for conceiving more radical ideas. If you were a manufacturer of spectacles in the 1950s and you focused on the problems of users, you might introduce all manner of improvements such as lighter frames or scratch-proof lenses. But if you concentrated on the limitations of the spectacles then you would almost certainly have missed the opportunity to find a different and lateral solution to the customers' problems. You would not have thought of contact lenses or laser eye treatment.

When Travis Kalanick could not get a taxi in Paris in 2009 he thought about the issue. Most of us would have asked, 'How can we get more taxis?' He ignored the taxi shortage, looked at the bigger picture and asked a different question. 'What if we could harness the capacity of all the drivers in Paris who would give me a lift for payment?' He founded Uber.

Hotel companies focused on improving their hotels by analysing the problems. The company Airbnb was founded in 2008 by Brian Chesky, Nathan Blecharczyk and Joe Gebbia. They ignored the problems with hotels and started completely afresh. They designed a marketplace for sellers and buyers of lodgings. They did not build any hotels. They built a website and an app. Airbnb is a shortened version of its original name, AirBedandBreakfast.com.

Every problem is an opportunity for innovation. Don't get sucked into the detail of the problem. Think laterally and bypass the problem altogether.

50
Music without music

Vulfpeck is an American funk band based in Ann Arbor, Michigan. It was founded in 2011 by Jack Stratton. The band wanted to organize a tour for their small but loyal fan base. The problem was that they had no money to fund it. The traditional approaches to this issue were to raise money by crowdfunding or selling tickets in advance or selling enough downloads. These were all difficult, so the band came up with a crazy idea, a hack to exploit a loophole in the royalty model of Spotify, the major music streaming site.

In 2014 Vulfpeck released an album called Sleepify. It contained 10 silent tracks, each of about 31 seconds. The album contains no audible sound! They published it on Spotify and asked their fans to leave it running overnight on a continuous loop. The name Sleepify reflects the idea that you play it while you sleep. Spotify pays artists a tiny sum for each track played for at least 30 seconds. Spotify is funded through advertising and subscriptions. The fans responded ardently and there were hundreds of thousands of plays. Vulfpeck earned around $20,000 in royalties from Spotify and sure enough, in September 2014 they put on the tour. It covered six major cities across the US from New York to San Francisco. Admission was free. It was called the Sleepify Tour and garnered the band enormous attention and good will.

This is the list of the tracks on the Sleepify album:

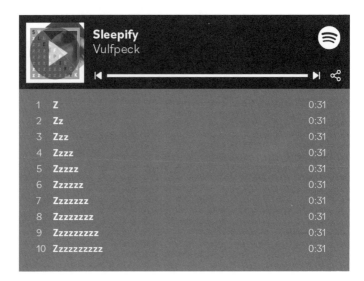

The album was given a droll review in *The Guardian* by Tim Jonze who remarked, 'The opening track Z certainly sets the tone, a subtle, intriguing work that teases the listener as to what may come next. It's followed by Zz and Zzz which continue along similar lyrical themes while staying true to Sleepify's overriding minimalist aesthetic.'[40]

The album's innovative royalty-generating scheme received worldwide press coverage, from Brazil to Russia. Spotify reacted with good humour. They called the idea a 'clever stunt' and paid the royalties due, but they pulled the album after seven weeks and then changed their terms of service.

What could be more lateral than a music album that contains no music?

51
Lateral marketing: The benefits of being outrageous

Today we are bombarded with messages from every quarter. So it is hard to be heard. A lateral way to draw attention to your creative idea is to be outrageously provocative.

Reverend Jonathan Swift was a prominent and satirical Anglo-Irish author, best known for *Gulliver's Travels*. In 1729 he published an essay entitled *A Modest Proposal*, in which he suggested that the poor should sell their children to the rich for them to eat. He wrote: 'A healthy young child is a delicious, nutritious and healthy food, whether cooked, roasted, baked or boiled.' He then listed the economic and social benefits. A great many people were outraged. Some took it seriously. It was only later in the essay that it became clear that Swift intended to provoke his readers. He then outlined the reforms he was proposing to improve the plight of the poor.

Swift's shocking provocation was justified. His *Proposal* had a profound impact. A proposal for sober and conventional reforms would have gone unnoticed. Swift wanted a quick reaction to a radical change. He tried his luck. He ignored the criticism. He took a risk and it paid off.

In 2007 the New South Wales Road Traffic Authority ran a controversial but successful marketing campaign against speeding. Previous campaigns featuring accidents and the dangers of speeding had had little effect. The new TV advertising campaign showed women shaking their little finger – a gesture used to symbolize a small penis – as speeding male motorists raced past.[41] The gesture caught on and this edgy campaign has won many awards. You can see the advert on YouTube.

The advert attracted complaints of sexism but was very effective – about 60 per cent of young men said the ad had made them ponder their driving habits. 'Speeding. No one thinks big of you' took the top prize for the most effective ad in Australia. It was praised for saving lives as well as $264 million in accident-related hospital costs. When conventional approaches fail it is time to try something radical and lateral – like challenging the masculinity of young speeding drivers.

People are easily offended; they get upset very quickly. So we tend to avoid controversy – to be polite, harmless and bland. But maybe it is worth upsetting people to break through and get our message across. In 2010 the betting company Paddy Power shocked the UK with a TV commercial featuring blind footballers playing with a ball containing bells. A cat with a bell around its neck wanders on to the pitch and is accidentally kicked out of the ground and into a tree by one of the players. The commentator says, 'We can't get the cat back, but if you place a bet with Paddy Power, you can get your money back.' This advert received a record number of complaints from viewers. Many complaints were from cat lovers and from older women. But Paddy Power didn't care. Because the advert amused and resonated with their target market – young men.

In 2013, there was a national scandal. Horse meat was found in various ground meat products. The English were horrified. You never eat horses in England. Paddy Power seized the moment. To exploit the contaminated meat scandal, they published a book of horse-meat recipes with their annual financial results. Their slogan was 'From stable to table'. Most people saw the funny side and the message got through.

For light subjects, humour and controversy go well together. But it is important to evaluate your audience. Who's going to be upset? It is very dangerous to outrage religious fundamentalists or extremist dictators but annoying old ladies who love cats – this is a reasonable risk.

Brazen marketing is cheap, but it takes courage, creativity and speed. It can then generate extensive coverage and send a message that you are agile and bold. But isn't this kind of marketing likely to annoy some customers? The answer is yes. Bland marketing does not upset anyone but no one remembers it.

Edgy marketing can annoy but will be memorable. If no one complains about your ad, it may be too bland.

In our world you have to do something extraordinary to be heard. If you have an important message to convey, assess the risks, consider using humour or provocation. Eschew the obvious. Be frank, controversial, even outrageous.

52
Lateral marketing – Topical mischief

On 19 October 2016 Brad Pitt and Angelina Jolie announced their split. It was big news all around the world. Seventy-two hours later, on 22 October, Norwegian Airlines announced a new campaign for inexpensive flights from London to LA with the message

> *Actor. LA. Newly single. Seeks like-minded partner with GSOH.*

They then released a print ad with the three-word headline 'Brad is single', next to the cost of a flight to LA. This cheeky campaign went viral and generated enormous coverage from all quarters. In an article in *Campaign* magazine, the VP of Marketing at Norwegian Air said, 'Real-time marketing presented us with an opportunity to quickly demonstrate our brand personality so we developed a playful ad – with the simple caption "Brad is single". The public received the ad with the humour it was intended and it has now gone viral.'[42]

In the 2004 European Football Championships England played Portugal in the quarter-final. England's Sol Campbell scored a fine goal which the Swiss referee, Urs Meier, disallowed. England went on to lose on penalties. English fans were outraged. The morning after the match Asda Opticians put out a press release announcing free eye tests for Swiss nationals in Britain.[43] It was an audacious piece of topical publicity. Some bright spark spotted the opportunity, and some senior marketing executive promptly authorized the impudent release. Very few companies are agile enough to initiate a bold piece of topical marketing in a couple of hours. Typically, such a decision has to go through lengthy approvals from risk-averse departments.

On 1 April 1998, Burger King announced the release of the new Left-handed Hamburger. The chain published a full-page advertisement in *USA Today* announcing the new menu item. The Left-Handed Whopper was designed especially for the 32 million Americans who are left-handed. All the whopper ingredients and condiments were rotated through 180 degrees. Thousands of customers went into restaurants to order the item while other customers insisted that they wanted their traditional right-handed hamburger. The next day Burger King issued a press release revealing that the Left-Handed Whopper was a hoax. The company garnered much good will and publicity with the stunt.

As mentioned in the previous chapter, Paddy Power in 2013 grabbed the opportunity of the horse-meat scandal to release a cookbook of horse-meat recipes. It was a highly mischievous move which gained much coverage.

Topical and cheeky marketing does not cost much money, but it takes courage, creativity and speed. It can then yield widespread coverage and sends a message that you are agile and bold.

But does this kind of marketing risk upsetting some clients? The answer should be yes. Of course, you do not set out to cause offence – unless perhaps you are Ryanair. In an interview for *Campaign* magazine, Ryanair's CEO Michael O'Leary said, 'Negative publicity sells more seats than positive publicity.'[44] Do not worry about your brand being tarnished by some mischievous campaign; worry about it being forgotten in the overload of information that is out there.

If your marketing budget is stretched, then try a dose of topical mischief. It is a lateral way to make a real impact.

53
Transplant an idea

An important lateral thinking technique is to take an idea from one field and plant in a completely different one. It is something we saw in the workshop brainstorm method called Similes.

Jorge Odón is an Argentinian car mechanic who in 2006 invented a simple device which could save the lives of millions of mothers and babies. He was shown a YouTube video of a trick to remove a cork from inside a bottle. The secret is to insert a plastic bag into the bottle, inflate the bag around the cork and then pull it out. He had a brainwave – he could use the same principle that extracted the cork from the bottle to extract a baby during a difficult childbirth. He developed the idea and discussed it with people – most of whom thought he was crazy. But he persisted. He patented the concept and gained the support of the World Health Organization. His device is now in use saving lives in many countries. He took an idea from a puzzle and applied to a problem in health care.

In 1916 a young American scientist and inventor called Clarence Birdseye went to Canada as a fur trader. He noticed that people kept their fish frozen in the ice in winter and the fish did not deteriorate. When he returned to the US, he developed this idea and in due course he started the frozen food industry.

Alexander Graham Bell studied the workings of the human ear. He adapted the idea of the diaphragm in the eardrum to create the vibrating diaphragm of the telephone.

Henry Ford copied the idea of the assembly line after he saw it in use in a meat-packing factory. He transplanted the idea into automobile manufacturing and transformed the industry. Later, Ray Kroc copied this idea from car factories and applied it to his restaurant chain, McDonald's, to develop the fast-food business.

Helen Barnett Diserens was a chemist working for the Mum deodorant company. She wanted to find a new way to apply a liquid. She copied the idea of a ballpoint pen and adapted it to create the roll-on deodorant.

The Danish architect Jørn Utzon won the Pritzker Prize, architecture's highest honour, for his creation of the Sydney Opera House, one of the most iconic buildings in the world. He based the design on the sails of sailing boats.

Two students at Stanford University in 1996 were looking for a way to assess the importance of webpages. They borrowed an idea from academia where the importance of a research paper is measured by how many other papers reference it. Larry Page and Sergey Brin had to download the entire internet at the time on to the Stanford server in order to use this concept to calculate the number of incoming links to each page. They had stumbled on to a powerful way of ranking pages and searching for them. They developed this idea into Google.

Lateral thinking is about finding new ways to solve problems. The challenge you face right now is similar to many other problems that people have faced in the past – in different times and environments. So look for similar issues in different arenas – the arts, entertainment, sport, military, medicine, education, architecture and so on. The wealth of creative ideas out there is legion and some of them can be transplanted into your field.

54
Café culture

Cafés have long been places of innovation and lateral thinking. Café owners have sought to differentiate themselves by creating novel spaces to attract customers. There are many hybrid cafés that mix coffee with barber shops, bookshops, bicycle repair shops or lawyers' offices. There are innovative business models and creative environments. Here are a few notable examples.

The Manuscript Writing Café in Koenji, Tokyo has a sign in its window: 'This is a café exclusively for those who are writing.' It has three rules.

1 Customers must initially declare the nature of their writing project, the number of words required and the deadline.

2 Every hour the proprietor checks on your progress.

3 You cannot leave until you reach your goal.

Writers sit at narrow counters, separated by plastic screens. They drink tea or coffee and work on their laptops. There is no music or other distraction.

'We don't have food or fancy roast beans,' says Takuya Kawai, the café's proprietor. 'The service we provide is concentration.'

It is the ideal place for a very specific demographic: writers under pressure who do not want to work from home, university or office.[45]

Meow Parlour in New York is a cat café. Cat lovers can drink their coffee in the company of the many feline residents. The cats can be stroked, cuddled and even adopted. This coffee shop also offers many gift items for cat fans and their pets.

Marmite opened a pop-up café in Soho, London, selling Marmite-based snacks and coffee. It has a unique way to pay – 'by sentiment'. When you arrive you enter your social media profiles into an app which analyses whether you are a 'lover' or a 'hater'. If your tweets and posts are mostly positive, then your Marmite on toast and coffee are free. If the app finds that you have been cynical, critical or nasty then you are charged full price. The app is called a Love-O-Meter. It is a fun experience for a group of friends who are active on social media to see who are the lovers and who are the haters.[46]

The Ziferblat chain of coffee shops has turned the business model around. The coffee and biscuits are free; the customer pays for time spent there on a per-minute basis. They describe themselves as anti-cafés. They offer fast WiFi connection, endless refills of your tea or coffee and a good working environment. You are charged for your time only. The chain started in Russia. The word *zifferblatt* means clockface in both German and Russian.[47]

Walter's Coffee Roastery in Istanbul was inspired by the TV series *Breaking Bad*. It is based on a chemistry lab and features many things from the show. It includes a huge periodic table on one wall, with science beakers and laboratory glassware for coffee mugs. Some of the staff wear yellow jumpsuits and the café offers false blue crystal meth-covered cupcakes. Ideal for fans of *Breaking Bad* and its lead character Walter White.[48]

Next time you need a lateral idea go and slowly sip a drink in a café – preferably one that is quirky and stimulating. It might be just the spur you need.

55

What's cooking?

As with cafés, restaurants offer great opportunities for creativity, innovation and lateral thinking. The more enterprising restauranteurs are always looking for clever ways to differentiate themselves. Obviously, they can do all manner of things with their cuisine and menu choices but they can also innovate with their location, appearance, business model and customer experience. Here are some that stand out.

Karen's Diner in Sydney, Australia encourages its staff to be rude to customers and to give poor service. In return customers are expected to complain, vent their anger and release pent-up frustrations. You can have a good meal (eventually) and a good argument. On their website they state, 'We hate good service. This will be the most fun you've had eating burgers, ever.'

The Disaster Café in Lloret de Mar, Spain offered clients the opportunity to experience a simulated earthquake measuring 7.8 on the Richter scale. While dining on international cuisine guests were also offered landslides and alien visitations. Great for groups.

The Macaroni Grill restaurant in San Antonio, Texas was busy at weekends but there was very little traffic in the early part of the week. The owner decided that one Monday or Tuesday every month all the food would be free but he did not announce which day. People constantly called to ask,

'Is tonight the night?' They found out when they arrived. Word spread and business increased.

The Labassin Waterfall Restaurant in San Pablo, Philippines is built into a beautiful natural waterfall. Guests sit barefoot with the water running around their feet and ankles for a unique experience.

S'Baggers in Nuremberg, Germany claims to be the world's first and only rollercoaster restaurant. There are no serving staff. You order on the pads provided and your meal slides right to your table on winding metal tracks.

The Bird's Nest Restaurant in Soneva Kiri Eco in Thailand is built as a series of bird's nests. They are in trees some 16 feet above ground. Waiters use purpose-built zip lines to deliver your food and drink orders.

The Ithaa Restaurant in the Maldives takes the opposite approach. It is built into the ocean, 16 feet below sea level, with a glass dome so that guests can enjoy their meals while surrounded by tropical fish. It claims to be the world's first all-glass undersea restaurant and was award the title of 'most beautiful restaurant in the world by the New York *Daily News*.

At the Kinderkookcafe in Amsterdam, Netherlands all the staff are children aged under 13. They prepare and cook the food, serve at your table and take your payment. Parents can enjoy the meals that their children have created. All are welcome but it is not open on school days!

56

Weird combinations

If you search the internet for 'weird food combination' you get hundreds of hits. Strange concoctions of different foods seem to be a favourite topic of bloggers and video makers. Here are some combinations they recommend you try:

- bacon and chocolate
- french fries and ice cream
- peanut butter and pickle
- salami and grapes
- raspberry jam with scrambled eggs
- chocolate and cheese pizza
- vanilla ice cream with soy sauce

They are modern examples of a phenomenon which has been around for a long time – marrying ideas. Most innovations are not completely new. They are combinations or adaptations of existing ideas.

A strong contender for the title of the greatest invention of all time is the printing press, created by Johannes Gutenberg in 1450 in Strasbourg. Before this invention books had been laboriously copied out by hand or stamped out with woodblocks. Gutenberg combined two ideas to invent a method of printing with moveable type. He married the flexibility of a coin punch with the power of a wine press. His invention transformed the spread of knowledge and ideas throughout the Western world. It was a key enabler of the Reformation, the Renaissance and the Scientific Revolution.

In 1972 a US patent for the wheeled suitcase was granted to Bernard Sadow, the owner of the company US Luggage. He attached a strap and four castors to a suitcase and persuaded Macy's department store to stock the product. Initially there was some resistance to the idea because men thought it unmanly to wheel a suitcase rather than carry it. Nowadays the suitcase without wheels is the rarity. What are the wheels you can put on your suitcase? What can you add to your product or service to make it better for customers?

Try combining your main product or service with a range of foreign concepts and see what you get. By putting together toys and management training, Lego was able to conceive a new corporate strategy technique whereby management teams build business models using Lego blocks. By combining the worlds of pharmaceuticals and fashion, L'Oréal has carved out a distinctive and successful strategy.

Take a product and think of an absurd way to make it work. Trevor Baylis was the English inventor who conceived the clockwork radio. What a strange combination! Radios need electricity and clockwork is a mechanical method. Surely batteries or mains electricity are better ways to power a radio. However, in the developing world batteries are expensive and mains electricity is unreliable. Baylis built a reliable radio that people could wind up by hand. It has transformed the availability of information in many of the poorest regions of the Earth.

You can apply the same process to combinations of partners and think of diverse individuals or organizations who could work with you. Combining your different skills could create an original approach to the market. Here are some examples:

- Lego Group and Levi's partnered to create a collection which included hoodies, jeans, jackets, hats and T-shirts. Each item has a patch where you can clip in Lego pieces.

- Pavarotti performed with the Irish rock band U2. They brought together disparate audiences who might never have considered such an alternative musical genre. Similarly Ed Sheeran appeared with Andrea Bocelli.

- Mercedes-Benz and Swatch combined to create the revolutionary Smart Car. A prestige carmaker and a fashion watchmaker came up with the most innovative town car ever seen.

- In 2020 Gucci and Disney announced a Micky Mouse-themed collection of collectible items including T-shirts, bomber jackets, bags and accessories.

Nearly every new idea is a synthesis of other ideas. So a great way to generate ideas is to force combinational possibilities. Get your team together and brainstorm how you could mix your products with those from wildly different sources. Take it to the extreme. How could you combine your key concept with random products, services, places, personalities, etc? The more bizarre the combination the more original the ideas that are triggered.

Study how your customers use your products or services. Do they use them with other products? Is there a combination you could create that would make things easier for your customers? Just like the drinks company who innovated with a ready-mixed gin and tonic.

57
What if your boss is risk-averse?

A common problem for the lateral thinker at work is a boss who just isn't interested in new ideas. They focus on doing the job in the way they have always done it and they don't like trying anything new. What can you do? Here are some approaches that can prove helpful.

1. Understand their objectives and motivations

Selling an idea is like selling any other product. You have to understand the needs, motives and priorities of the customer. What are your boss's 'hot buttons'? What are the issues that really worry them? Are they motivated by pride, ego, money, career advancement, power, recognition, or do they want an easy life? If you can discover their goals and motivations, then you can try to present your idea in a way that plays to these aims. Stress the outcomes of the idea that will help your boss.

2. Understand their decision-making style

How does your boss make decisions? Do they prefer numbers, reference from trusted sources, evidence of proof elsewhere, avoidance of risk, logic or emotion? Do they make quick decisions, or do they like to chew things over for a while?

3. Align your idea with corporate objectives

It will help if you can show that your idea fits with current corporate objectives. Show clearly how the suggestion will benefit the larger organization.

4. Choose the right time

Don't barge into your boss's office at the end of a hectic day and buttonhole them with your great idea. Chances are they will simply say no. Instead ask them for some time to discuss an important issue and mention the benefit. 'Can you spare 20 minutes first thing tomorrow morning to review an idea to improve departmental productivity?' Don't give the idea away now – you need their full attention to cover it properly.

5. If they are risk-averse sell risk avoidance

Sell the benefits of the idea and try to match them to the needs and priorities of your boss. Show that you have thought about the risks, costs and downsides. If your boss is risk-averse then stress the risks of not implementing the idea. 'If we don't seize this opportunity now, other departments could step in ahead of us and gain an advantage.'

6. Don't ask for approval, ask for suggestions

With some bosses it is better not to present a fully formed plan but simply to introduce the concept and ask for their input and advice. Do this if they prefer to discuss things and shape them rather than review and approve. This way you can let them form their version of the idea and claim the credit. You will have the quiet satisfaction of knowing that it came from you.

7. Build a coalition of supporters

With some ideas it is better to gain some initial support before asking for approval. Who do you need on your side to help push the idea through? Have a chat with them first. 'I checked with Betty in IT and with Bob in HR and they agreed that we can resource this if it is approved.'

8. Try the company suggestions scheme

If your boss shows no interest (and probably never will) then you can always try the official suggestions scheme. The evaluator may see the merit of the idea. In any event it is registered and that means it can be discussed in the open.

9. Build it anyway

This is the ultimate act of confidence and bravado. Do it in your own time as a 'skunk works' project and then you can demonstrate the prototype to garner support. Present it as a fait accompli and boldly shrug off any notions that it needed prior approval.

10. Quit

It is said that people leave bosses not jobs. If your boss is making your life a misery, then move elsewhere – preferably upward but a lateral move can be good for a lateral thinker. There is considerable evidence that middle managers block innovations. So if you want your idea to succeed you will need a clever way of gaining approval. Keep trying; your organization needs innovators!

58
Become an ideas carrier

As a lateral thinker you can increase your success at work if you can become an ideas carrier, someone who identifies, collects and communicates fresh ideas for other people's business challenges. If you work in an office you can do this for your colleagues, your boss or the people who report to you. If you are a consultant or salesperson, you can do this for your customers. If you are a buyer you can do it for your suppliers. In every case you can build your relationship by helping the other person solve their problems.

Let's say you work in sales. Think of your most important customers. What are their most pressing business challenges? What are the top priorities and the worries that keep them awake at night? Forget for the moment about trying to sell them your products; focus instead on their problems and issues. Now as you go about the rest of your business look out for ideas that might help. Maybe when you are speaking to a colleague or another customer or reading you will see something that might possibly be helpful. Send your customer an email with the link or a letter with the magazine clipping and a note saying, 'I was thinking of the issue we discussed and saw this idea that I thought might help.' Your customer may adopt or reject the idea for all sorts of reasons but the very act of making the suggestion serves some valuable purposes. First, it reminds them about you. Secondly it shows that you are interested in solving their problems and not just in selling your products. Thirdly it gives you a good reason for a follow-up telephone call: 'Was the idea useful?' Similar considerations apply if you supply an idea for a manager in another department of the company. It raises your profile and shows you are a constructive, helpful kind of person. These are the sorts of considerations that can help your image and career.

To become an ideas carrier you need three things:

1 An interest in the challenges that other people face. You can find out about these with intelligent, sensitive questions. Most people are happy to open up about the business issues they face.

2 An open, inquiring mind. You need to be on the lookout for new ways to do things and fresh ideas.

3 The willingness to offer the ideas, put them into context and communicate them in a positive manner.

Become known as someone who is always ready with suggestions and fresh ideas. You can build your reputation with a combination of three things. First, your understanding of the needs of the key people you meet. Secondly your industry knowledge and contacts with other people. Thirdly your imagination, lateral thinking and ability to spot connections. You can construct your own unique selling proposition with this combination. By carrying innovative ideas from one place to another you can help your customers, build your relationships and advance your career.

59

Go back to the future

A lateral thinking technique for leaders is to travel forward in time. If you are planning a major change, a big initiative, a new product launch or something really innovative then try writing a future news story. Imagine that the project has been a surprisingly big success. A reporter in a major newspaper or on TV files a glowing report. Write it up. It should include:

- How unexpectedly successful it has been.
- The remarkable benefits that it has brought to people.
- Quotes from enthusiastic users.
- The strong initial opposition from people and how they were brought around.
- Some technical or logistical difficulties that were faced and overcome.
- How the idea is now being adopted, copied and developed.

Write the report and then share it with your team or whoever is working with you on the project. It should be amusing and provocative. More importantly it should help you focus on the benefits of your plan and the challenges you have to overcome. It will provide a fruitful basis for discussion and should be highly motivational for everyone involved.

When Anne Mulcahy was appointed CEO of Xerox in 2001, many people were surprised, including Mulcahy herself. She had never run a company before and had little financial experience, having worked mainly in sales and human resources functions. Xerox faced huge financial problems and the stock price fell 15 per cent on news of her appointment. The financial market had little confidence in her ability to turn around the stumbling giant.

Her advisers urged her to declare bankruptcy because of the mountain of debt. But instead she implemented a dramatic recovery plan. Capital spending was cut by half and general expenses by one third. But she ignored advice to cut research and development. She invested in innovation. She sold unprofitable units, eliminated 28,000 jobs and slashed administrative expenses while protecting Sales and R&D. She saved the company.

During the whole painful process she placed great emphasis on communication. In order to promote her vision for the future of Xerox she created a fictitious *Wall Street Journal* article describing Xerox in the year 2005. 'We outlined the things we hoped to accomplish as though we had already achieved them,' said Mulcahy. 'We included performance metrics, even quotes from Wall Street analysts. It was really our vision of what we wanted the company to become.' The article was sent to every employee and people understood where the company was headed.[49]

The company's turnaround was built on restructuring and the introduction of innovative products and services. In 2008 Mulcahy was named CEO of the Year by *Chief Executive* magazine.

The converse approach is to anticipate failure. Time travel with a pre-mortem. A post-mortem establishes the cause of death; a pre-mortem anticipates it. Say you are working on an important bid for a major contract. Late in the day call your team together and tell them, 'I just got a phone call from the client today and he told us that we lost – he didn't tell us why.' You then ask people why they think you lost. The team will come up with all manner of issues that you had not thought of before. Now you prioritize those points and use them to significantly improve your proposal. This sneaky method also works with big projects or change initiatives. Imagine the project has failed and then model all the things that could have gone wrong. It will help you to anticipate and counteract problems and impediments.

Don't stay in the present, be prepared to go back to the future.

60
Don't reject ideas with *Yes but*

Lateral thinkers are always inquisitive. They know that new ideas are only partly formed so they prefer to explore rather than reject.

One of the exercises on my Creative Leadership workshop runs like this. People in pairs have short conversations. In the first conversation one person makes a suggestion for something new that could be done for customers (say). The second person replies with an objection. They start their sentence, 'Yes but...' The first person then rebuts the objection with another sentence starting, 'Yes but...' They carry on, ensuring that every sentence starts with the words 'Yes but...' After a couple of minutes they stop and then begin a second conversation. One person starts with a suggestion for something new that could be done for employees (say). The second person adds to the idea with a sentence beginning, 'Yes and...' The first person responds with a sentence starting, 'Yes and...' and so it goes on. In the first conversation every sentence after the first starts, 'Yes but...' In the second every sentence after the first starts, 'Yes and...'

The results are instructive. Typically, the first conversation spirals down into an argument with no agreement. In a business setting the more powerful person would usually win. The second conversation goes to all sorts of creative and unusual places. It is fun and leads to interesting ideas.

I then ask the delegates which conversation type is more common in their organization. It is always the 'Yes but...' When we say, 'Yes but...' we are really saying, 'No.' It is the quick, negative, normal response to fresh ideas in the office. Einstein said that every truly great idea initially appears absurd. The more offbeat and radical the idea the easier it is to find fault with. We can show how clever we are by pointing out some of its obvious flaws. The typical responses to a creative suggestion might be:

- Yes but it would cost too much.
- Yes but the boss would never agree to that.
- Yes but we are too busy right now.
- Yes but we tried something similar last year and it did not work.

When we say, 'Yes and...' we start playing with the idea and exploring its possibilities. 'Yes and...' does not mean immediate approval; it means, 'Let's see where this goes.'

Amazon has directly addressed the issue of knee-jerk negative reactions. They have implemented what CEO Jeff Bezos calls 'The Institutional Yes.' If you are a manager at Amazon and one of your people comes to you with a suggestion your initial answer must be Yes. If you want to say No then you must write a report on why you are stopping this idea. Amazon has made it much easier to say Yes rather than No so that more ideas are tried and implemented.

If your default response is 'Yes but...' then try saying 'Yes and...' Start a quiet revolution in your business by exploring crazy ideas rather than immediately rejecting them.

61
Experiment, experiment, experiment

There is no point in being a lateral thinker if all your great ideas remain as abstract concepts. If you want to change the world, then you need to turn some of them into action.

Think of a big organization; maybe you work for one. What would the response be if I asked the leader of this organization this question: 'Would you like your people to try out their ideas for better ways to meet the needs of customers?'

Most leaders would respond in the affirmative – perhaps with a guarded 'Within reason'. They would like to see people trying to find new and better ways to do things on their own initiative. They know that if you want a truly innovative organization then you have to release and empower your people to try new things as and when they see fit. This means encouraging people to seize the initiative and try new things in the areas where they have responsibility. Many companies do this. Facebook even lets programmers try experiments with the live site under some conditions. Most CEOs get this. They see the need for innovation and are frustrated with the rate of change. They would like to see more experimentation in order to increase business agility and entrepreneurial activity.

Now consider this question: 'Are people empowered to try out their ideas?'

Here you get some interesting and divergent answers. Often top leaders think that the answer is Yes. But people lower down the same organization will give a negative reply saying something like, 'No. They expect us to get on with our jobs and it would be risky to try something new which might fail.' Employees think that experimentation and risk-taking are discouraged. They may have heard stories of people whose careers ended when they tried something which went badly wrong. This perception may be wrong but, in corporate culture, perception is reality.

We know that experiments can lead to great innovations. Ted Hoff invented the microprocessor for Intel when his boss let him try a crazy idea. Thomas Edison famously carried out tens of thousands of experiments. Jorge Odón experimented to find a new way to help childbirth. Paul MacCready flew, crashed and adapted his way to make the first effective human-powered plane.

Most experiments will fail – in one sense – but you will learn stuff that you did not know before. Incidentally here is a list of some successful products that were the results of experiments and accidents.

- corn flakes
- Viagra
- Coca-Cola
- Jacuzzi
- microwave oven
- saccharine
- Play-Doh
- Crisps (potato chips)
- penicillin

- chocolate chip cookies
- Slinky
- pacemaker
- ink-jet printer
- Post-it Notes
- text messaging

How can you foster a climate of constructive experimentation? First, give people broad objectives. Define the ends but not the means. Secondly, empower people to experiment. They should keep their boss appraised of their plans and given the time and space to them. Third, encourage people to share experiences. Treat 'failure' as a learning opportunity. Fourth, change your attitude to risk; don't minimize risk, manage it.

If you want an agile, creative and innovative business then the motto is experiment, experiment, experiment.

62
Welcome failure

As mentioned in the previous chapter, experimentation involves failure and many great innovations have resulted from experiments which 'failed'. Yet the word *failure* carries many negative connotations. In our society we applaud success and disdain failure. The lateral thinker has to turn this notion upside down. They should welcome failure and be wary of success. Failure is an essential part of the exploration and trial of new ideas, whereas success can breed complacency, self-satisfaction and aversion to risk.

Why does Rafael Nadal (or any other great tennis player) serve double faults? Every double fault is a failure – it gives a precious point to his opponent. He could easily cut out all double faults by slowing down his second serve to ensure that it lands safely in the service box. Yet in most long matches Nadal, like most other top players, will serve at least four double faults.

Clearly the tennis champion has made a careful calculation of the trade-off between being bold or cautious on his second serve. He knows that if he makes his serves safe he will make the returns easier for his opponent. He wants to win a high percentage of points on his serve and use it as an attacking tactic. He is quite prepared to lose some points as double faults if it means that most of the time his serves are difficult to return. There is an optimum number of double faults that a tennis player should serve in a match and the number is not zero.

The same principle applies to us in our enterprises. Caution can be an enemy of success. If every new thing that we try works it almost certainly means that we are not being bold enough. We should take some courageous initiatives. We should sometimes fail. We should serve some double faults.

What innovations have you tried in the last three months? Make a list. How many succeeded and how many failed? For those that failed, why did they fail? What lessons can you learn? Obviously you aim for success and you want to win. But there will be failures on the road to success. If you cut out the possibility of failure then you limit your chances of success.

Similar principles apply for leaders. They should encourage an element of failure in the actions of their people. This is especially true if you want to change a corporate culture that is comfortable and risk-averse into one that is adventurous and entrepreneurial – fine words are not enough. The leader needs to send some powerful signals through deeds.

Very often the best way to test an idea is not to analyse it but to try it. The organization that implements lots of ideas will most likely have many failures but the chances are, it will reap some mighty successes too. By trying numerous initiatives we improve our chances that one of them will be a star. As Tom Kelley of IDEO puts it, 'Fail often to succeed sooner.'

What makes Silicon Valley so successful as the engine of high-tech growth? It is the Darwinian process of failure. Author Mike Malone puts it like this: 'Outsiders think of Silicon Valley as a success, but it is, in truth, a graveyard.

Failure is Silicon Valley's greatest strength. Every failed product or enterprise is a lesson stored in the collective memory. We don't stigmatize failure; we admire it. Venture capitalists like to see a little failure in the résumés of entrepreneurs.'

Here are some tips for succeeding through failure:

Understand the difference between two kinds of failure. There is an honourable failure when a trial of something new did not succeed. There is an incompetent failure when an operation failed because of faults in individual performance.

The lessons from failures should be shared and used as starting points for improvement.

Recognize that when you give people freedom to succeed, you give them freedom to fail.

Talk about your failures and what you learnt from them.

Publicly praise someone who tried something that failed.

Let people know that honourable failures will not be criticized.

Tata showcases over 3,000 product innovations in its annual awards. It has a *Dare to Try* category which comprises 'courageous attempts that did not achieve the desired results but have potential for success'. A spokesperson said, 'Too much of our culture was about good news. Our meetings were designed to talk about good news. Now, the whole paradigm is changing. People are passionately telling us what has failed and more importantly, what they have learnt about why it failed.'[50]

Lateral thinkers in leadership positions encourage experimentation and failure with words and actions. If you want people to be daring and entrepreneurial then you should recognize and reward heroic failures.

Part Six
Lateral thinking in society

63
Cool lateral ideas

There are a myriad of lateral ideas in action to solve every-day problems. We now take them for granted but when they were first proposed they may have been seen as risky, silly or impractical. Here is a random selection of some of my favourites.

Problem: *Customers were waiting in line to be served by a busy assistant in a grocery shop.*

Lateral idea: Michael Cullen turned the shop around and let customers serve themselves. He created the world's first supermarket, the King Kullen store in Queens, New York, in 1930.

Problem: *Naughty children are being disruptive on a trip.*

Lateral idea: Take a bag of the children's favourite sweets (unwrapped). Tell the children they will share whatever sweets are left. Every time a child is badly behaved throw a sweet out of the window. Peer pressure and loss aversion will see to it that the kids behave.[51]

Problem: *Thieves were stealing the lead from church roofs.*

Lateral idea: An enterprising priest installed hives in the church roof with a warning at the door 'Beware of Bees in the Roof Space.' Criminals were deterred and the honey produced by the bees was sold at the church bazaar.

Problem: *A Chinese woman gave birth to four identical quadruplet boys. It was nearly impossible for her or anyone else to tell them apart. What to do when they went to school?*

Lateral idea: She had the hair on their heads shaved to display the numbers 1, 2, 3, 4.[52]

Problem: *A couple were going on holiday and were worried about a power cut ruining all the food in their freezer. There had been electricity power cuts both long and short in their area. If there were a long power cut and then the power was restored their food would have been defrosted long enough to go off, but it would be frozen on their return. How could they tell?*

Lateral idea: They placed a coin on top of a big ice block in a bowl in their freezer. If on their return the coin was still at the top, then there had been no power cut or a very short one. If the coin was underneath the ice in the bowl, then there had been a long power cut and their frozen food was suspect.

Problem: *A female rock star wants to gain significant PR exposure without spending a fortune.*

Lateral idea 1: Adele entered an Adele impersonation contest in disguise. After the other singers gave their best imitation, a woman called Jenny came on stage and sang flawlessly. The looks on the faces of the contestants as they realized they were in the presence of their idol made a wonderful TV programme which became a big hit.

Lateral idea 2: Lady Gaga appeared at an awards ceremony in a dress made of meat. She knew it would be controversial, so she had prepared an explanation about it being a protest against exploitation. The news coverage was prodigious.

Problem: *Washing machines are very heavy and therefore costly to transport. They contain a heavy concrete block which keeps the unit stable in the spin cycle.*

Lateral idea: Replace the concrete block with a large empty plastic box. When the washing machine arrives at the user's house the box is filled with water. This provides the weight to stabilize the machine. Replacing concrete with water saves significant cost and CO_2.[53]

Problem: *Some people might vote more than once in elections.*

Lateral idea: Apply a vegetable dye to the thumb of each person who votes.

Problem: *Two glass tumblers are stuck together – one inside the other.*

Lateral idea: Put cold water into the inner glass and a bowl of hot water around the outer glass. The outer glass will expand and the two are easily freed.

Problem: *The mining company De Beers mined diamonds which were used as industrial drill bits. What should they do with the many diamonds that were unsuitable or too small for drill bits?*

Lateral idea: De Beers put diamonds to a new use when they created the concept of engagement rings. It opened up a large new market for them.

Problem: *Graffiti artists who were known to authorities were told they would be prosecuted if they painted graffiti on city walls.*

Lateral idea: They did the opposite of applying something to the wall; they removed something. They used stencils and detergents on dirty walls. Their pictures and messages were left where the walls were cleaned. They were safe from prosecution because there was no ordinance against cleaning a dirty wall.

Problem: *A Swiss city found that pigeons were swarming over its tourist sites. Tourists were asked not to feed the pigeons, but this advice was ignored and did not help.*

Lateral idea: The city tourist office gave out bags of food for tourists to feed the pigeons. The food contained a contraceptive which did not harm the pigeons but stopped them from reproducing.

64

Lateral thinking in the fight against crime

On the night of Sunday 19 December 2004, two groups of armed men, masquerading as police officers, arrived at the homes of Christopher Ward and Kevin McMullan in Belfast. Both men were officials of the Northern Bank, one of the largest banks in Northern Ireland. Their families were taken hostage and the men were told to go into work as normal the next day.

Ward and McMullan followed instructions and gave the robbers entry to the bank the next evening. The gang got away with a huge haul – around £25 million in cash. Most of it was in Northern Bank banknotes. The hostages were released unharmed. Over the following months and years arrests were made and some stolen money was recovered. Police recovered £2 million during raids in Cork and Dublin. Around $100,000 in US banknotes was recovered from a toilet in the police athletic association's country club. Although many people blamed the IRA for the raid the identity of the culprits has never been established and the crime remains unsolved.

However, following the raid, officials at the bank and the government did some lateral thinking. The bank recalled all of its banknotes in circulation – around £300 million in total. It reissued new notes in different colours with a new logo and new serial numbers. The first of these new notes entered circulation in March 2005. Anyone holding old bank notes had to bring them in to be changed – and that is a big problem if you are holding millions of stolen banknotes. The authorities could not catch the robbers or recover all of the loot but they did manage to make much of the haul worthless.

In 2022 a Michigan woman, Wendy Lynn Wein, 52, pleaded guilty to solicitation of murder and using a computer to commit a crime.[54] She was sentenced to between seven and twenty years in prison. She had used the website rentahitman.com, a bogus site for people who want to hire an assassin. Wein had asked the website owner, who called himself Guido Fanelli, to put her in touch with a 'field operative' who could murder her estranged husband. She agreed a fee of $5,000 if the assassination were carried out. Her details were handed over to the police. The website was founded by Bob Innes, a businessman from California. The information he has provided to the authorities has so far helped save the lives of 150 people. He registered the domain name as something of a joke in 2005 but traffic gradually increased. Rentahitman.com has a contact form for clients. It claims to have won industry awards and that it complies with HIPPA, the 'Hitmen Information Privacy and Protection Act of 1964'. There are also fake testimonials from satisfied customers, including from one woman who says she's 'ready to mingle' after having her cheating husband bumped off.[55]

Another example of lateral thinking in law enforcement was provided when the FBI and the Australian Federal Police collaborated in 2019 to create a fake encrypted chat platform to catch criminals. The platform, Anom, was promoted to crooks, enabling law enforcement to listen in on their conversations. According to a Europol press release, Anom was remarkably successful and grew to include messages from over 300 criminal syndicates in over 100 countries and including many international drug gangs. In 2021, after reviewing 27 million messages from criminals, police forces in various countries swooped and arrested 800 people. They also seized eight tons of cocaine, 250 firearms, 55 luxury vehicles and over $48 million in various worldwide currencies and cryptocurrencies.[56]

Smart criminals use lateral thinking to find new ways to rob and defraud. We need to use lateral thinking in the fight against them.

65
A lateral way to expose war crimes

The English journalist and blogger Eliot Higgins became interested in open-source methods in 2011 when he wanted to authenticate video clips from war zones and crime sites. He found that you could use satellite imagery to check the locations of videos, but it needed many pairs of eyes to review all the possible comparisons. In 2012 in his blog *Brown Moses*, he posted articles with videos from the civil war in Syria. He and his collaborators analysed hundreds of short videos and were able to authenticate their locations using geolocation techniques. He researched the weapons used and was able to show that the Syrian government of Bashar al-Assad was using chemical weapons and cluster bombs.

In 2014 he founded Bellingcat as a journalistic group which would investigate war crimes and major incidents using open-source intelligence (OSINT). They would analyse thousands of documents and posts in the public domain to accurately identify and verify information. Initially all members of the group were unpaid volunteers. The name Bellingcat comes from the old tale of mice who complain about a cat. The mice agree that it would be great if they could hang a bell round the neck of the cat – but no mouse dares to try to do it. Belling the cat means bringing aggressors out of the shadows.

Bellingcat's first major success was its investigation into the downing of Malaysia Airlines Flight 17 which was shot down on 17 July 2014 while flying over Ukraine. All 283 passengers and 15 crew were killed. Through painstaking research Higgins and his team were able to show that Russian forces were responsible for the atrocity by using a Buk missile launcher. They tracked the progress of the Buk using photos from many sources on the internet and by using Google Earth to verify locations and in some cases the length of shadows to identify time of day. Their findings were later confirmed by the Dutch-led international joint investigation team.

Bellingcat identified the coordinates of an Islamic State training camp and the site where an American journalist was killed. They went on to expose atrocities in Syria, Yemen and Cameroon. In a major coup, Bellingcat discovered and revealed the identities of the three Russian GRU agents responsible for the poisoning of Sergei Skripal in the city of Salisbury in the UK in 2018. Their continued success has enraged the Kremlin, which regularly denounces Bellingcat for 'disinformation' and being a tool of Western intelligence services. In fact, they are fully independent and their funding comes from grants, donations and selling workshops which train people in the skills of open-source investigations.

During the Russian invasion of Ukraine in 2022 Bellingcat has been very active and shown the use of cluster bombs. The Bellingcat website was blocked for Russian users.

Bellingcat has received many awards and honours and it has changed how news and intelligence agencies gather and verify stories using OSINT methods. These are mighty achievements by Higgins and a group of crowdsourcing amateurs sitting at their computers.

66
Acknowledge the value of ignorance and doubt

We value knowledge and certainty and disdain ignorance and doubt. Ignorant is an adjective of derision. Perhaps we overvalue knowledge and underestimate the power of ignorance; or should I say the awareness of ignorance? Why is this? Because knowledge can breed certainty, hubris and closed minds. We need to be open-minded and even doubtful about our knowledge because what was true yesterday may no longer be true today. The expert advice given to residents during the 2017 Grenfell fire in London, where 72 people died, was to stay in their flats. It was a fatal misdirection.

In the Middle Ages the authority of the Church and the Bible was unchallenged. There was a certainty in the order of things and the reason for things. The revolutions of the Reformation and the Renaissance came about when people began to doubt things. The scientific revolution was based on the realization that we were profoundly ignorant about how the universe really worked. Indeed, the scientific method is based on challenging knowledge. Every scientific principle is a theory that can be questioned. Newton's Laws and the consequent view of the universe were the bedrock of mechanics and physics for centuries until challenged and updated by Einstein's theory of relativity.

We seem to prefer political leaders who are sure of themselves and their policies. Any political leader who expressed doubts about themselves or their plans would be derided as wishy-washy. The author John Adair says that the most important sentence for a leader to say is: 'I admit that I was wrong.'[57] But on the rare occasions when political leaders change their minds they are accused of flip-flopping, of doing a U-turn or of lacking conviction. But there is no value in having convictions if they are for wrong-headed ideas. Joseph Stalin and Robert Mugabe just kept pressing on with the wrong precepts. Their obstinate and single-minded approaches impoverished their peoples. We need leaders who are open to doubts, receptive to new evidence and prepared to change direction.

Mikhail Gorbachev was a dedicated Communist party officer who rose to be leader of the USSR. He saw the many problems of the Soviet system and changed his mind, introducing the radical policies of perestroika and glasnost. This led to independence for the former Soviet satellite states and the fall of the Berlin Wall in 1989.

F W De Klerk was the last President of apartheid South Africa. He had been a strong advocate of apartheid but changed his view and took the courageous decision to release Nelson Mandela in 1990 and start the transition to a multi-racial society.

We all suffer from confirmation bias, the tendency to search for, recall and prefer information that confirms our pre-existing beliefs. The effect is stronger for emotionally charged issues and for deeply held positions. It leads us to interpret ambiguous evidence as supporting our beliefs. For example, when a mass shooting occurs in the US proponents of gun control see it as proof of the need for restrictions on gun ownership, whereas opponents of gun control see the same incident as evidence for the need for more people to carry guns so as to quickly shoot the assailant. Similarly, when there is savage snowstorm some people see it as clear evidence of climate change and others as proof that global warming is a myth.

Confirmation bias leads to overconfidence in personal beliefs despite contrary evidence. In 1992 Rachel Nickell was brutally murdered on Wimbledon Common in London. The police brought in an expert who constructed a psychological profile of the killer. The police found a suspect, Colin Stagg, who walked his dog on the Common and who fitted the profile. There was very little evidence that he had had anything to do with the crime, but the police became convinced that he was the murderer and they laid an elaborate 'honey pot' plan to encourage him to confess. This did not work but they brought him to trial where the judge threw the case out. Eventually, in 2008, Robert Knapper was convicted of the killing of Rachel Nickell. It is clear that once the police officers became convinced that Stagg was guilty they rejected contrary evidence and confirmation bias set in. They redoubled their efforts to build a case against him.

Knowledge is a good thing, but we have to recognize that our knowledge is partial. It is constrained by our point of view and our internal biases. Leaders are at their most dangerous when they are certain in their knowledge that they are right. The world is moving fast and some of our beliefs might be outdated or just plain wrong. We have to be cautious about experts, certainty and righteous self-confidence. Lateral thinkers acknowledge their ignorance, listen to contrarian views and ponder over doubts.

67
Lateral thinking in nature

The 17-year cicada has the longest known life cycle of any insect. In the US large broods of this species appear on time every 17 years. When a tiny cicada nymph emerges from its egg it burrows into the ground, where it lives for 17 years. After this exact time, it waits until the ground temperature reaches 18° C and then emerges in huge numbers. It lives for only four to six more weeks, in which time it eats and mates and the female lays eggs so the long cycle can start again. Why 17 years? No one knows for sure, but it is interesting to note that 17 is a prime number. Cicadas appear to be a delicacy for many predators including birds, mice, lizards and, in China, people. Say the life cycle of the cicada was 12 years. Then any predator with a life cycle of 2, 3, 4, 6 or 12 years would reproduce in numbers just as the cicadas were emerging. But the prime number 17 is only divisible by itself and one.

Evolution has been at work for so long and tried so many variants that it has produced some amazingly clever and unusual life and survival strategies. In that regard the methods used can look remarkably lateral.

Female cuckoos do not make a nest, but rather they watch for another pair of birds to build a suitable nest in which to lay their eggs. When the cuckoo is ready, she will take an egg out of the chosen nest and eat it. She will lay her own in its place. The cuckoo can lay up to 25 eggs in a season in other birds' nests. The host bird incubates the intruder cuckoo egg alongside its own. But the cuckoo chick hatches after just twelve days and is then ruthlessly selfish. It will push other eggs or chicks out of the nest to ensure that it receives all the food from its step-parents. The cuckoo chick often grows to be much larger than its step-parents. It then flies off.

The porcupine fish or pufferfish is slow moving but not an easy prey. When threatened by a predator, it can inflate its body using air and water. It can blow itself up to several times its normal size and extend its sharp points out up to 5 cm. It also contains deadly toxins.

The wood frog has a highly unusual self-freezing technique. In winter 40 per cent of the frog's body can turn to ice. It holds glucose in its liver, which acts as a type of antifreeze. So the frog stays alive while appearing to be frozen solid. In this state it stops breathing, its blood ceases flowing and its heart stops. When the temperature rises the frog comes back to life.

The African termite builds amazing mud structures which are water-proof and can reach 9 metres high. These mounds have many ventilation passages which improve air flow and keep the inside environment relatively cool even in very hot weather. Engineers and architects have studied termite mound design to help us build homes that can stay cool without air-conditioning.

One of the best sources of fresh ideas is the natural world. Nature solves problems in all sorts of clever ways so it can often provide an innovative solution for your business problem. Alexander Graham Bell based the design of the telephone on the workings of the human ear. The diaphragm in a phone is similar to the diaphragm in the ear. When doctors wanted to design a better hypodermic needle they looked to nature for inspiration and based their innovative design on the proboscis of a mosquito. The design of Pringles potato chips is copied from wet leaves which fold together in a pleasing curve.

As mentioned elsewhere, George de Mestral was the Swiss engineer who went for a walk with his dog. On his return he noticed that many plant burrs adhered strongly to his clothes and his dog's fur. He studied the burrs under a microscope and saw that they worked with little hooks. He copied this idea in his invention of Velcro – which is now used as a fastener all over the world.

Artists have long looked to nature for inspiration – particularly in art and music. So have doctors, engineers and designers. In its myriad ways nature can point out novel ideas and clever solutions to everyday problems.

68
Lateral thinking in art

Art has many examples of novel ideas, sweeping new movements, lateral turns of direction and outrageous creations. The artist Marcel Duchamp took a urinal, signed it, turned it upside down and submitted it to an exhibition at an eminent art society in New York in 1917. The company's board of directors rejected it on the grounds that it was not art. Duchamp, who was a member of the board of directors, resigned in protest. A storm of debate and controversy ensued. Duchamp won the argument and huge publicity. In 2004, the urinal was voted the most influential work of art of the 20th century. He firmly established the principle that it is the intention and choice of the artist that make a work of art.

Let's consider one of the greatest and most lateral turning points in the history of art, surrealism.

This was a development in which artists depicted unnerving, illogical and unexpected scenes in order to enable the unconscious mind to express itself. One of its leaders, André Breton, described the purpose of surrealism as 'to resolve the previously contradictory conditions of dream and reality into an absolute reality, a super-reality'.[58] It started in Paris after the First World War and spread across many genres including painting, writing, theatre, filmmaking, fashion and photography.

The subversive idea underlying surrealism was to turn human experience on its head and to replace a rational view of the world with something fantastic, strange and uncanny – the stuff of dreams. The word means beyond reality.

One of the leading figures in surrealism was the Spaniard Salvador Dalí. His most celebrated painting is entitled *The Persistence of Memory*, which features images of soft, melting pocket watches. It was painted in 1931. The art historian Dawn Adès wrote, 'The soft watches are an unconscious symbol of the relativity of space and time, a Surrealist meditation on the collapse of our notions of a fixed cosmic order.'[59] This suggests that Dalí was reflecting an understanding of Einstein's new theory of special relativity. When he was asked if this was true Dalí replied in typical fashion that the painting was in fact inspired by a perception of a Camembert cheese melting in the sun.

One clock in the picture is covered in ants, which Dalí used to imply decay. Another clock features a fly which appears to cast a human shadow. You can see this remarkable painting in the Museum of Modern Art in New York.

Dalí worked in many media and produced a plethora of bizarre and striking pieces of art. A famous example was his lobster telephone consisting of a real telephone with a bright pink lobster made of plaster. Another notable piece is the Mae West Lips Sofa. As the name suggests it is a surrealist sculpture in the form of a red sofa shaped like the lips of the actress Mae West.

There have been powerful and revolutionary trends in the history of art from Gothic to the Renaissance to Impressionism to Cubism to pop art. But surely none is more radical or provocative than surrealism. It is an inspiration to lateral thinkers everywhere.

69
Remote collaboration

In 2001 two musicians, Ben Gibbard and Jimmy Tambrello, wanted to collaborate on some new compositions. The problem was that they lived hundreds of miles apart at opposite ends of America's west coast. Tamborello composed some rhythms (or 'beats') and sent them to Gibbard on CD by post. Gibbard added some instrumentals and vocals and returned the arrangements to his partner. Back and forth the CDs went with edits and additions until eventually they had enough material for an album. In acknowledgement of their method they called themselves The Postal Service and the album they released in 2003 was called *Give Up*. It was well received and sold over one million copies. Three singles were released from it. You can hear them on Spotify.

In 2003, the United States Postal Service (USPS) sent the band a cease and desist letter, stating that the band's name was an infringement of its trademark. But the two sides came to a mutually beneficial agreement. The USPS allowed the band use of the trademark in exchange for promoting USPS and a performance at its annual Executive Conference. The USPS even sold the band's CDs on its website.

There have been many other such long-range collaborations. Lil Nas X, an American rapper, bought a beat from Youngkio, a Dutch musician, to create the track 'Old Town Road'. The two had never met but the song went on to top the Billboard charts in 2019. It is an example of an innovative new blend – country rap.

The lesson is clear. Creative people do not have to be in the same room in order to collaborate on lateral ideas and innovations. How can you harness this idea in the age of Zoom and Teams meetings? Here is a brainstorm method I call 'The Postal Service'. You gather a group of say six to ten people on a Zoom meeting and explain the challenge: we need great ideas to tackle this problem. You articulate broadly what a good solution would look like and express the challenge in terms of an outcome: 'How could we…?'

Working individually (and remotely), people then go away, think about the issue and write down four separate ideas to tackle it. I encourage people to include one safe idea, one creative idea and one crazy idea. The ideas are then distributed – four to each participant. Person A gets an idea from persons B, C, D and E, and so on. People receive four ideas from four different people. Each person selects the two most promising ideas and then adds details and suggestions to make them better.

The group now reassembles in threes – typically in Zoom breakout rooms. Each group of three shares their proposals – six in all. They discuss these in detail and select the best one or two to present back. At this stage they can adapt, combine or improve the ideas. The whole group then meets on video conference and the best ideas are presented and discussed. The group votes to select the ideas that will go forward for trial and implementation.

We need to work remotely and we need to innovate, so why not combine the two? Some people think better on their own and some people spark off others in groups. This method offers both approaches. I recommend it to you.

70
Mental health hacks

Many people suffer from mental health issues such as depression or anxiety. Here are some creative ideas to help you combat these ailments and to maintain and strengthen your mental health.

Go outside

We spend much of our lives inside buildings, whether offices, shops or homes. Go for a walk or a run in the country and experience a change for the body and the mind. As the UK NHS site says, 'Walking is simple, free and one of the easiest ways to get more active, lose weight and become healthier.' The change of environment and closeness to nature can provide a mental stimulus. Many people find that they get their best ideas away from the office and while walking.

Perform a random act of kindness

Being good to other people makes us feel better about ourselves. According to research by Liudmila Titova and Kennon Sheldon, 'Happiness comes from trying to make others feel good, rather than oneself.'[60] In five studies they found that a strategy of trying to make other happier was more beneficial than a strategy of trying to make yourself happy. Try doing something generous and unexpected – even for a stranger.

Volunteer

Help others by volunteering. Use your skills to help young people, old people or people in need. According to the Mayo Clinic, volunteer activities keep people moving and thinking at the same time. Research has found that volunteering among adults aged 60 and over provided benefits to physical and mental health. Research has also shown that volunteering leads to lower rates of depression and anxiety, especially for people 65 and older.[61]

Watch a comedy film

Take time to watch one of your favourite funny movies – slapstick, juvenile humour seems to work best. 'If you are having a sad moment or need a boost of energy, watching something funny can be a great pick-me-up,' said LeAnn DeHoff, the clinical director at the Lux Center of Counseling and Education. 'Smiling and laughing are positive for your mental health.'

Write down a list of things you are thankful for

Make a list of all the things that you are grateful for. Start with basic things like your health, the roof over your head, your education. Then record some of your positive achievements. The longer the list the better – it will put your problems into perspective. Writing the list can help you build self-esteem and reduce stress. Find something to be thankful for every day.

Imagine positive motives in others

When someone accelerates past you in traffic make up a story about them. Maybe they are taking a sick child to hospital. When you do this your anger and stress immediately dissipate. Think good thoughts about other people and you will feel better yourself.

Call an old friend

Be sure to spend time with your good friends but also find time to renew old friendships. Call your best friend from school and have a chat about old times and new. We are so busy with today's problems that it is easy to let valuable friendships slide away. It is worth making even small efforts to keep them.

Ask for help

Men in particular tend to harbour problems and they often feel that asking for help is a sign of weakness. But if a friend asked them to help they would jump at the chance. Friends and colleagues can be a source of support if you share with them. People want to help each other. Ask for help before the problem overwhelms you.

Accept criticism

Be thick-skinned. Don't bristle when someone says something disconcerting about you. If it is a joke laugh it off. If it is a criticism then consider there is probably at least a grain of truth in it so use it as a prompt for improvement. Try not to see it as a denunciation of you as a person but as a comment on your behaviour. If they are in a bad mood then it is their problem, not yours.

Read poetry

A 2021 study of hospitalized children found that providing opportunities for them to read and write poetry reduced their fear, sadness, anger, worry and fatigue.[62] Poetry allows us to see the world and its troubles through the ideas of others. We share their feelings. A poem can provide comfort and lift us when we feel depressed or stressed. Some people find that writing poetry helps them to cope.

71
Summary and conclusions

We have reviewed a battery of lateral thinking principles, examples, stories, methods and puzzles. Here is a brief summary of some of the key points that the book is designed to express.

1 Lateral thinking is an approach to problem solving which is open to everyone and in all fields.

2 For most challenges there is an opportunity to find a new and different solution. We should explore a legion of possibilities rather than accepting the first idea or the conventional approach.

3 We all make assumptions every day and in every situation, but these assumptions can seriously limit our ability to conceive new possibilities.

4 The best way to challenge assumptions is by asking fundamental, even childlike questions such as 'Why are we doing this? What if the opposite were true? Is there a better way?'

5 We can be inspired by and learn lessons from the great thinkers, inventors and innovators of the past.

6 Before trying to come up with solutions we should first strive to fully understand the problem. Tools like Six Serving Men can help.

7 We can use a range of workshop methods to help our

lateral thinking including the Random Word, Similes or Roll the Dice.

8 Six Thinking Hats and the Disney Method can help make our meetings faster, more productive and more open to consider fresh ideas.

9 Many people are risk-averse and prone to conformity and groupthink. We should be aware of these tendencies and be prepared to combat them in different and subtle ways.

10 We can harness the random to help us think laterally and see new possibilities.

11 If we want to put lateral ideas into action then we must try many experiments.

12 We need to welcome failure as a learning experience – we should learn to fly, crash and adapt.

You are now invited to approach situations with an open mind, challenge conventions and think the unthinkable. Take inspiration from the stories, think differently and sidestep the obvious. Throughout society we need smarter solutions to problems large and small. We need lateral thinkers. So let's join the revolution and get to work.

ANSWERS

Riddles (pages 84–85)

1 It only takes one brick to complete the house

2 February – it has the fewest days.

3 No time at all – the 10 people already built it.

4 There are a great many more of them.

5 We do not bury living people in England.

6 A haircut (or a shave).

7 Their rifles are long enough already.

8 Lunch, dinner and supper.

9 It is very hard to crack a concrete floor.

10 Your feet off the floor.

11 Twelve: the second of January, the second of February…

12 A lid.

How many did you get?

Lateral thinking puzzles (pages 93–94)

Mountains ahead

The plane is sitting on the ground at the airport in Denver, Colorado, which is one mile above sea level.

The key

The woman's husband was an habitual sleep-walker. He had previously opened the front door in his sleep and walked out into the road. She placed the key in the bucket of cold water so that if he reached in to the water to get it the cold sensation would waken him.

The damaged car

A few minutes earlier the man had been the driver in a fatal hit and run accident. He drove to the car park and then made it look as though the car had been stolen and vandalized. He then phoned the police to report his car stolen. (This is a true incident. He was later caught and sent to prison.)

The blanket mystery

He was an Indian brave who sent smoke signals to warn of the approach of a troop of cavalry.

The seven-year itch

The woman had been shipwrecked. She found a pirate's treasure but was not rescued for seven years.

Sand trap

This incident reputedly occurred during the war between Israel and Egypt. Because of import duties, Mercedes cars were much more expensive in Egypt than in Israel. When Israel seized vast tracts of the Sinai desert, a clever Israeli businessman realized that the land would have to be handed back to Egypt after the war. By burying the cars he effectively exported them without them moving when the border shifted! His Egyptian associate subsequently sold them at a handsome profit.

Mathematical problems (page 137)

1 It is possible to calculate proportions using algebra. But the lateral solution is as follows. Both glasses have the same volume at the end of the process, so any water that is not in the water glass must be in the wine glass and vice versa. There is as much water in the wine glass as wine in the waterglass.

2 The tedious way to solve this is to count the number of knockout ties in each round. However, with 79 entries there is one winner and 78 losers. Each match produces one loser so there are 78 games.

3 Every day our snail gains one foot in elevation so you might think the answer is 30 days to climb out of the well. But that is not correct! After 27 days and nights, the snail is 27 feet up from the bottom of the well. On the 28th day, it climbs the remaining three feet to the top of the well, so the correct answer is 28 days.

NOTES

1 Edward de Bono. *The Use of Lateral Thinking*, Jonathan Cape, 1967

2 Edward de Bono. *Sur/Petition*, Macmillan, 1992

3 Matthew Syed. *Rebel Ideas: The power of thinking differently*, John Murray, 2021

4 Irving Janis. *Groupthink: Psychological studies of policy decisions and fiascoes*, Houghton Mifflin, 1982

5 Randall Lane. *You Only Have to Be Right Once: The rise of the instant billionaires behind Spotify, Airbnb, WhatsApp and 13 other amazing startups*, Penguin, 2016

6 Job Creators – The Entrepreneurs Network

7 Arnobio Morelix, Chris Jackson and Inara Tareque. Want to be like Silicon Valley? Welcome immigrant entrepreneurs, Kauffman Foundation, 7 October 2016

8 Stuart Anderson. Immigrants, Nobel Prizes and the American Dream, *Forbes*, 14 October 2020

9 Emma Elsworthy. Curious children ask 73 questions each day, *The Independent*, 3 December 2017

10 Alistair Cox. Why you shouldn't always just 'Google it', LinkedIn, 2 November 2020

11 Peter Drucker. *The Peter F. Drucker Reader: Selected articles from the father of modern management thinking*, Harvard Business Review Press, 2016

12 Malcolm Gladwell. Viewpoint: Could one man have shortened the Vietnam War?, BBC News, 8 July 2013

13 Dmitry Shvidkovsky. *Russian Architecture and the West*, Yale University Press, 2007

14 Pagan Kennedy. *Inventology: How we dream up things that change the world*, Houghton Mifflin, 2016

15 Edward de Bono. *Six Thinking Hats*. Little Brown and Company, 1985. Six Thinking Hats is a trademark of the De Bono Company

16 Steffan Powell. Playtime: Is it time we took 'play' more seriously?, BBC, 13 January 2022

17 Paul Sloane and Des MacHale. *Great Lateral Thinking Puzzles*, Sterling Publishing, 1994

18 Gary Hamel. *Leading the Revolution*, Harvard Business School Press, 2003

19 Selin Malkoc and Gabriela Tonietto. The calendar mindset: Scheduling takes the fun out and puts the work in, *Journal of Marketing Research*, 1 December 2016

20 Taiwan car thieves use birds to collect ransom, *Journal of Commerce*, 23 October 1991

21 Tom Nichols. *The Death of Expertise*, Oxford University Press, 2017

22 Kyle Dropp, Joshua D Kertzer and Thomas Zeitzoff. The less Americans know about Ukraine's location, the more they want US to intervene, *Washington Post*, 7 April 2014

23 Tessa Berenson. A lot of americans support bombing the fictional country from *Aladdin, Time*, 18 December 2015

24 Elizabeth Suhay and James N Druckman. The politics of science: Political values and the production, communication, and reception of scientific knowledge, *Annals of the American Academy of Political and Social Science*, 8 February 2015

25 Eric Abrahamson and David H Freedman. *A Perfect Mess: The hidden benefits of disorder*, Little Brown, 2006

26 Kathleen D Vohs, Joseph P Redden and Ryan Rahinel. Physical order produces healthy choices, generosity, and conventionality, whereas disorder produces creativity, *Psychological Science*, 1 August 2013

27 Tim Harford. *Messy: How to be creative and resilient in a tidy-minded world*, Abacus, 2018

28 Katherine W Phillips, Katie A Liljenquist and Margaret A Neale. Is the pain worth the gain? The advantages and liabilities of

agreeing with socially distinct newcomers, *Personality and Social Psychology Bulletin*, 29 December 2008

29 Paul Sloane and Des MacHale. *Mathematical Lateral Thinking Puzzles*, Sterling Publishing, 2015

30 Ernest Dichter. *Handbook of Consumer Motivations*, McGraw-Hill, 1964

31 Daniel Boffey. Swedish firm deploys crows to pick up cigarette butts, *The Guardian*, 1 February 2022

32 Tucker Archer. 5 fast facts your need to know about Sergey Brin, Heavy.com, 8 April 2021

33 Tony Hsieh. *Delivering Happiness*, Grand Central, 2010

34 Tony Hsieh. 'Delivering happiness': What poker taught me about business, *HuffPost*, 26 May 2010

35 Alex Pentland. *Social Physics: How social networks can make us smarter*, Penguin, 2015

36 Bruce Daisley. *The Joy of Work: 30 ways to fix your work culture and fall in love with your job again*, Random House, 2020

37 University of Minnesota. Ceiling height can affect how a person thinks, feels and acts, *ScienceDaily*, 25 April 2007

38 Rebecca Hinds. Why meeting table room shapes matter, *Inc.*, 13 October 2017

39 David Niven. *It's Not About the Shark: How to solve unsolvable problems*, St Martin's Press, 2014

40 Tim Jonze. How to make money from Spotify by streaming silence, *The Guardian*, 19 March 2014

41 Julian Lee. RTA gave the finger to acclaimed pinkie ad, *Sydney Morning Herald*, 31 August 2009

42 Stine Steffensen Borke. The story behind Norwegian Air's 'Brad is single' ad, *Campaign*, 29 September 2016

43 Free eye tests for the Swiss, *Bolton News*, 28 June 2004

44 Loulla-Mae Eleftheriou-Smith. Ryanair's Michael O'Leary: 'Short of committing murder, bad publicity sells more seats', *Campaign*, 1 August 2013

45 Richard Lloyd Parry. Deadline looming? This writers' café won't let you leave till you're done, *Sunday Times*, 24 April 2022

[46] Isabelle Aron. Marmite is opening a pop-up café where 'lovers' eat for free and 'haters' have to pay, *Time Out*, 4 August 2015

[47] Vicky Baker. London's first pay-per-minute cafe: will the idea catch on? *The Guardian*, 8 January 2014

[48] Julia Brucculieri. This 'Breaking Bad' coffee shop will feed your caffeine addiction, *HuffPost*, 28 July 2015

[49] Lisa Vollmer. Anne Mulcahy: The keys to turnaround at Xerox, *Stanford Business*, 1 December 2004

[50] Kevin Freidberg, Jackie Freidberg and Dain Dunston. *Nanovation: How a little car can teach the world to think big and act bold*, Nelson, 2011

[51] Kevin Kelly, 103 bits of advice I wish I had known, kk.org, 28 April 2022

[52] Daniel Miller. Hair's looking at you kids: Chinese quadruplets have numbers shaved onto their heads so teacher can tell them apart, *Daily Mail*, 7 September 2012

[53] Paul Ridden. Concrete-free washing machines are lighter to transport, just as good in a spin, New Atlas, 4 August 2017

[54] Amber Ainsworth. Michigan woman who used Rent-A-Hitman in attempt to have ex-husband killed sentenced to prison, Fox 2 Detroit, 13 January 2022

[55] Natasha Wynarczyk. Spoof hitman website 'rentahitman.com' helps catch almost 150 would-be murderers, *Daily Mirror*, 9 January 2022

[56] 800 criminals arrested in biggest ever law enforcement operation against encrypted communication, Europol press release, 9 June 2021

[57] John Adair. *Effective Leadership*, Pan, 2009

[58] André Breton. *Surrealist Manifesto*, 1924

[59] Dawn Adès. *Dalí*, Thames and Hudson, 1982

[60] Liudmila Titova and Kennon M Sheldon. Happiness comes from trying to make others feel good, rather than oneself, *The Journal of Positive Psychology*, March 2021

[61] Angela Thoreson. Helping people, changing lives: 3 health benefits of volunteering, Mayo Clinic Health Care, 16 September 2021

[62] Anna Delamerced, Cia Panicker, Kristina Monteiro and Erica Y Chung. Effects of a poetry intervention on emotional wellbeing in hospitalized pediatric patients, *Hospital Pediatrics*, March 2021